We Are
The Freedom People

Sharing Our Stories, Creating A Vibrant America

Edited by Jennifer L. O'Donoghue & D'Ann Urbaniak Lesch

Foreword by Harry C. Boyte

Sentinel Printing Company

*Special thanks to Center for Democracy and Citizenship for allowing the time and space for this work to be done.

Sentinel Printing Company, St.Cloud, MN 56302

Photography: Joyce Yamamoto and Peter Leach
Design: Jane Sherman, By Design a student design studio
serving the University of Minnesota
Editors: Jennifer L O'Donoghue and D'Ann Lesch
Editing Assistance: Joyce Yamamoto

For more information contact:
Center for Democracy and Citizenship
130 Humphrey Center
301 19th Avenue South
Minneapolis, MN   55455
www.hhh.umn.edu/centers/cdc

"What is the freedom you love so well?"

"I guess now it ain't nothing but knowing how to say what I got up in my head."

—Ralph Ellison, The Invisible Man

Contents

* Names are pseudonyms.

FOREWORD

We are the Freedom People is a collection of stories, artfully wrought. The book explores meanings for our time of "great words" such as freedom. Over the last three years as I have worked with and learned from participants at Jane Addams School, I have found the stories inspiring and the concept of freedom that infuses the School useful and important.

This book recounts personal narratives of Hmong refugees (participants of Jane Addams School) who fled the Hill Country in Laos after the Communist takeover in 1975. Nan Skelton from the Center for Democracy and Citizenship helped to create the School in 1996, working with Nan Kari from the College of St. Catherine, John Wallace from the Philosophy Department at the University of Minnesota, and Sandy Fuller from Neighborhood House. They began with conversations with Hmong and Latino immigrants on the West Side of St. Paul to determine what such a nonformal "School" might look like. The partnership approach has continued since. The Jane Addams School opened "its doors" at Neighborhood House in the fall of 1996 as a combined community-based learning center and a place for public work initiatives. There, students from local universities and colleges join in mutual learning experiences with Hmong and Latino immigrants, community activists, Mormon missionaries, faculty from area colleges and others. From its beginning, the School has stressed reciprocal learning where "everyone is a learner, and everyone is a teacher."

I have come to see the Jane Addams School as a dramatic and powerful example of what might be called a "partnership approach" between colleges and communities, based on long-term, reciprocal, and mutually respectful relationships. Such partnerships offer many different stakeholders opportunities for creation and innovation. This book is a powerful and vivid example. Editors Jennifer O'Donoghue and D'Ann Lesch drew on their own rich experiences living abroad, learning about different cultures first and foremost through relationships with people, as they approached their work on this book. They felt it an important public document where the voices of Jane Addams School would be seen, heard, and valued.

The Center for Democracy and Citizenship involvement with the Jane Addams School has given us a laboratory to deepen and experiment with "public work," the core concept of the Center for Democracy and Citizenship. We define public work as "sustained, visible, serious effort by a diverse mix of ordinary people that creates things of lasting civic or public significance."

In addition to diverse learning projects, participants at the Jane Addams School have undertaken a wide range of public work projects, many intergenerational. Indeed, the creation of the School itself can be considered "public work." Such projects generate power and confidence and a feeling of stake in America. They have included a health and wellness festival organized by Latina women in health fields working with college students; public art on the West Side of St. Paul; and a cooperative farming program in which participants of all ages work and contribute their harvest to the Neighborhood House food shelf. School participants have worked with the regional Immigration and Naturalization Service (INS) to create a more respectful, collaborative relationship in order to improve the naturalization process. I have worked closely with Seng Yang and his group, Hmong Unity, a group of veterans who fought in "the secret war" against Communists in Laos during the Vietnam era, to press for American recognition of their contributions. This recognition was promised in the 1960s by the CIA, when they recruited the Hmong people to the war. To date the promise remains shamefully unkept. I feel strongly that the breech dishonors our nations word. We have enlisted many American-born college students and community groups in letter writing campaigns and organized meetings with representatives and senators in this effort. The issue of veteran recognition forms an undercurrent for all these stories because it is so central to the identity and history and culture of the Hmong. The passion Hmong feel about it was vividly illustrated by a group of young people, ages 8 to 14, who, with the help of others at the School, raised $5,000 to support six Hmong girls and four young adults on a trip to Washington in the summer of 1999 to press the case with political leaders.

The Jane Addams School has been a learning laboratory for many of us to think more deeply about freedom itself. For the Hmong, we discovered, "freedom" has been a guiding ideal and a practical struggle throughout thousands of years of their history, first in China against imperial power and then, for the ancestors of the Hmong in Minnesota, against colonial and communist authorities. The quest for freedom was the driving motivation for their long voyage away from the Laotian hill country and to the United States. Yet overwhelming and unanticipated new threats to freedom appeared on their arrival: dependencies on welfare and social service bureaucracies; racism; gang violence; dramatic clashes between generations of "Americanized" youth and elders shaped by a far different world; an American culture which often measures a person s worth simply by money and consumption levels. For American-born participants at the Jane Addams School, "freedom" was mostly taken for granted. Few would have pondered its "loss". The intensity of freedom for the Hmong has unearthed profound resonances in the word for all of us.

The meanings of freedom and its connection to power in the Jane Addams School also draw from its namesake, Jane Addams, the educator, democratic theorist, and political activist who guided the Hull House Settlement in Chicago for decades. Hull House was grounded in diverse immigrant cultures. Like the Jane Addams School, Hull House created space for educational and action projects, working "with" immigrants rather than delivering services "to" them.

The Jane Addams School similarly aims to "free the powers" of all its participants for contributions to democracy. It encourages public work, becoming itself a mediating institution which connects immigrants' everyday lives to the larger public world. Newcomers to America, and "old" Americans alike, gain a new sense of stake, ownership, pride, and belonging. They develop confidence that they can impact the larger world and the skills they need to do so. Through this process it makes freedom come to life with richness and multi-dimensionality. These are several themes of freedom that weave through this work:

1) New identities. As you will read in these pages, "freedom" for the Hmong means not simply freedom from oppressive power—a historic struggle of the Hmong people, dating far back to their struggles against Chinese imperial systems. It also means the freedom that comes with an integrated sense of self, in a world threatening to tear identity apart, especially between generations. The Jane Addams School forms a context for the struggle of Hmong young people to negotiate the tensions between "Hmong" and "American." The alchemy of the School has dissolved the forced choice between either-or, allowing the emergence of a third option, "Hmong-American."

2) Freedom as text, as well as context. The stories of the Hmong have tremendous impact on American-born students and others who work with them. Ordinary people—people who were illiterate, who were seen and defined as marginal, who were castigated and stigmatized—have amazing stories of stunning courage and passion for "freedom." Hmong stories of hardship, bravery, determination and vision powerfully make words like freedom come alive.

3) The uses of diversity. Freedom in the Jane Addams School sense, understood as the liberation of public energies, talents,

cultures for contribution to a vibrant democracy has generated an understanding of "diversity" that is different than conventional approaches. Usually, diversity is understood simply in racial and cultural terms, with a strongly moral element ("we should have more of this group, or that group"). Freedom as contribution highlights the diverse ideologies and views, as well as backgrounds and cultures, that are often useful for common public work. The School crosses partisan labels of left and right, Republican and Democrat, as well as huge cultural differences. It creates the space for people with an array of ideologies, backgrounds, interests, and cultures to work together around common projects and the theme of democracy.

The Jane Addams School is helping to pioneer a broad movement for civic revitalization that is stirring in our time. This movement may reshape American society. This book thus is a brilliant depiction of the Jane Addams School spirit and of its possibilities, alike.

What will it mean for the "we" who are fired by a vision of freedom to expand to include not only the Hmong, but Americans as a whole, once again? It is a question for us all.

Harry C. Boyte,
Co-Director, Center
for Democracy and
Citizenship

PREFACE

After three years of living, learning, and being with the Jane Addams School for Democracy we have a much keener sense of the possible. We—college and high school students, Hmong and Latino residents, faculty and staff—came together in the beginning from worlds that rarely crossed. Many college students had never said hello to a Hmong woman. Many Hmong high school students had never spoken to a college student. However, crossing worlds is not for the purpose of saying hello but rather to develop an ability to make radical shifts in thought, in life experiences and one's ability to respond.

Those of us at the Jane Addams School are now able to claim crossing worlds as part of our collective lived experience. We know that crossing worlds is part of the work of building a more vital democracy. To date we have begun to create a culture where college students from one end of the world have the freedom to self-interrogate, challenge, and change while at the same time Hmong and Latino residents from another world are beginning to discover and claim that same freedom. We have learned we need each other to make the crossing.

As we move forward, we also recognize that the continuance of memory is an integral part of the process. The work of telling stories, of remembering, is politically dynamic because the telling goes beyond anecdote and becomes survival. At the core is the survival of memory itself. In the words of Patricia Hampl, "Memory, for a small nation (or one denied sovereignty) is the nation."

In seeking refuge in this country, the Hmong people brought with them their memory. This book is a basic political act because it seeks to keep alive the language, the history and the culture of those gathered in its folds.

Nan Skelton

"Without Jane Addams School, I wouldn't have a place to create. I wouldn't be able to speak. I'd only be spoken to."

Terri Wilson, Winter 1998

Introduction

Struggling To Become Ourselves

Creating a Space for the Voices of the People

"Before all else, we see and listen and it is thanks to this that we understand." [1]

We Are the Freedom People grows out of more than two years of work at the Jane Addams School for Democracy. It chronicles the lives of individuals and of relationships. It is an attempt to tie together the stories and struggles of many people involved at the School. From disparate backgrounds, ranging from the mountains of Northeastern Laos to the streets of Yonkers, New York, we found our way to a common space and time. Together we have participated in an ongoing conversation reflecting our struggles to become ourselves and to (re)define what it means to be American. While growing out of the time and place of the School, the stories included here are not confined to that place. The School represents a space where relationships have developed and where a community has been cultivated. By participating in this community, we opened the doors for these conversations to take place.

The community created at the School is a living organism; it grows and changes with time. As such, the narratives in this book are both part of and products of the "lived experiences" of the people who tell them and the people who listen. For the stories are neither static, definitive, nor exhaustive. They grow from each individual through the web of relationships that continues to form and reform as our work together progresses. The stories capture a particular moment in the life of the storyteller and in the development of the relationship between listener and teller.

At first glance, the people in this book seem utterly dissimilar. There is great variety in life experiences, backgrounds, cultures, and ages (to name just a few) represented in this work. This book retells the stories of several Hmong women and men who escaped a war in Laos, came as refugees to this country, and struggle to make their way in an unfamiliar and often hostile environment. It illuminates the struggles of Hmong American high school students, many born in the US, as they work to form a "third identity" that incorporates their family backgrounds and their daily experiences in "mainstream" America. It recounts the struggles of Hmong, Latino, and European American college students to find their place in a society that presents few outlets for creativity and expression outside of the dominant "culture". It also presents the stories of older (beyond college-aged) "Americans"—university professors, social workers, and others—who have struggled for

---

1. Boal, Augusto. The Rainbow of Desire. New York: Routledge. p. 28. 1995.

years to resist being stifled by institutional and professional cultures.

Woven throughout these diverse stories is the common theme of freedom. This includes freedom from limitations, discrimination, oppression and even death. It is also the freedom to become more fully oneself, to have the power to create one's own life and world.

Working on this book helped us to see more clearly that what unites all of us is our common struggle to become ourselves, to create the worlds that we want, and to forge a new vision of what it means to be American.

The stories within this book reflect the tales of individuals working to craft their lives in opposition to dominant cultures—be they racial, ethnic, professional, academic, or consumer—that circumscribe this process. Indeed, the book itself is an attempt to create a space for our individual voices and identities to be seen and heard. This book grows out of the relationships that are the soul of the Jane Addams School and creates a public space where our stories are heard and valued. It is an insertion into what must be an ongoing, public discussion of who we are as Americans and what we could become.

Questioning Our Motives—Why's and How's of Telling

As interviewers, interviewees, and editors of this collection, we have been in a continuous process of reflecting on the importance and challenges of presenting the life stories of others. The first question to start with is why—why tell these stories? Why does this book have value and for whom? Questions that logically follow include the how's— how to collect the narratives, how to present them, how to work with multiple languages and translations? Perhaps the most important "how" question—how can we be accountable for the fact that our work will have effects that reach beyond our intentions?

When telling the stories of the Hmong parents and youth in particular, people who have not only had little opportunity or space to have their own voices heard, but have also become the exoticized objects of the "mainstream" media, how do we prevent these stories from reinforcing existing stereotypes? How can we make the voices of individuals heard without their becoming representative of an entire group of people?

"Autobiography, by its very nature, is an assertion of the power of the individual." [2]

The idea for this book came from individuals who through cooperative work are developing relationships with one another at the Jane Addams School. It is clear to all of us that there are amazing stories being told that need to be gathered. We have a strong belief in the

---

2. Rubin, Steven (ed.). Writing Our Lives: Autobiographies of American Jews. Philadelphia: The Jewish Publication Society. p. xxiv. 1991.

power of the telling, the power that comes when one has the space to define their own reality, to publicly share their stories with others.

Seeing Ourselves in the Mirror

Having a voice in a public setting offers validation of an individual's knowledge and experiences. The importance of this validation cannot be overemphasized. Adrienne Rich once said, "when someone...describes the world and you are not in it, there is a moment of psychic disequilibrium, as if you looked into a mirror and saw nothing."[3] This lack of reflection removes agency from and denies the reality of an individual. They are no longer subjects, but at best objects and at worst invisible. Therefore, it is imperative that individuals have the space to share their own voice, to see themselves reflected in the public mirror. Augosto Boal writes of this process, of denying an individual voice, in relation to theater:

> When the spectator herself comes on stage and carries out the action she has in mind, she does it in a manner which is personal, unique, and non-transferable, as she alone can do it, and as no artist can do it in her place. On stage the actor is an interpreter who, in the act of translating, plays false.[4]

PETER LEACH

3. Fu, Danling, My Trouble is My English: Asian Students and the American Dream. Westport: Boynton/Cook Publishing. p. 128. 1995.
4. Boal, Augusto. The Rainbow of Desire. New York: Routledge. p. 7. 1995.

[5]

Boal's description of the theater translates to everyday life. It speaks again to the importance of being able to share one's own story, without having it told as someone else would tell it. It points to the personal validity that can only come from having a public voice. Moreover, having a public "stage" for the telling of our stories allows us to "see ourselves as we see ourselves, and see ourselves as we are seen."[5] It offers the reflection that brings social validation.

This public validation of one's voice is the first step in building strength and capacity within an individual. From this, one can be moved to action in other areas. In fact, several community workers and educators have described the process of recovering or recognizing their voices and the role it played in their own development. Linda Stout describes the way that she found her voice in working to understand oppression. "Trusting my own voice," she writes, "meant overcoming both my fear of expressing my views and the feeling that I didn't deserve to be heard."[6] Developing this trust in her own experience was a critical step in her beginning to work in communities and to organize to effect social change. The telling is a public declaration that we deserve to be heard, that there is value in our stories.

Danling Fu also writes of the growth of her own voice as a learner and an educator. In her first educational program in the United States, she had learned to distrust herself and to squelch her own voice. When she joined a different community, one that welcomed her voice and ideas, she was transformed.

> I spoke first in a whispering voice and timid tone: many people had to lean forward in order to hear me. Gradually, with the encouragement of their interest and curiosity in whatever I said, my voice became louder and louder...[this] built my confidence, and overcame both my fear and my feeling of being an outsider.[7]

The community in which she was immersed played a critical role in her belief in her voice. Those around her and in relationship to her let her know that her story was welcomed and valued.

Moreover, respecting and listening to stories and experiences allows individuals to build on their past experiences. They are thus validated and strengthened. Rather than denying or feeling ashamed of their backgrounds, they come to respect that background and use it as a springboard for future action. One example of this comes from a first grade classroom in Baltimore, Maryland where a portion of each day's learning involved the sharing of the children's experiences. In large part, the learning that took place within this class came from these

5. Ibid., p. 26.
6. Stout, Linda. Bridging the Class Divide. Boston: Beacon Press. p. xiv. 1996.
7. Fu, Danling, My Trouble is My English: Asian Students and the American Dream. Westport: Boynton/Cook Publishing. p. 12. 1995.

daily recountings. "These accounts were taken seriously as contributions to the linguistic environment."[8] The stories, and thus the children's diverse realities, were celebrated, discussed, and incorporated into the daily learning.

Redefining Citizenship—Creating Alternative Realities

This example stands in stark contrast to the United States citizenship exam—a test that completely invalidates the unique life experiences of individuals. When the Jane Addams School first opened, the Hmong residents' learning desires were clear—they wanted to work with college students to prepare for the citizenship test. Therefore, we initially came together around the test, and it is around the test that we have since struggled to create a different reality, a reality that incorporates our authentic selves and recognizes the power inherent in the genuine relationships we develop through sharing those selves.

In many ways, passing the citizenship exam represents an official "entry permit" into the rights and responsibilities of naturalized citizenship in the United States. It offers a certain public recognition. To many Hmong residents, taking and passing the test is seen as a responsibility. As one Hmong woman stated:

> One night there was an American girl, a college student, who asked us why we are so concerned about the citizenship test. Why do we care so much, why are we working so hard, what's the big deal about it? And we thought, "Why is she even asking us these questions?" We think it's the least we can do to become part of this country, and we really want to do it. Even though you are old and your life is really hard and you've struggled through Laos and Thailand just to get here, when you get here, they say you should become a citizen, so you struggle to do it.[9]

Passing the test gives not only outside validation as members of this nation, but also safety. It removes fear of deportation, of withdrawal of welfare or social security benefits, and of denial of opportunities with which citizens are privileged. "Every day they talk about how they're going to cut all the Asians from assistance, and if you're not a citizen, you can't get assistance. It's not like people are using guns to fight, but it is the same as a war. There are the sounds of war, the voices of war."[10]Becoming a citizen, therefore, provides a perception of security for a people who have lived through so much tragedy and uncertainty.

However, this test serves as a prime example of what Lisa Lowe terms a "nationalist narrative." The exam "recognizes, recruits, and

8. Rose, Mike, Possible Lives: The Promise of Public Education in America. New York: Penguin USA. p. 137 1996.
9.Interview with Yer Vue Moua, 3/14/98
10. Ibid.

incorporates male subjects, while 'feminizing' and silencing the students who do not conform to that notion of patriotic subjectivity."[11]There are no women discussed in this "history" of the United States, only one person of color is named, and the only immigrants mentioned are the English. It is a lifeless piece of paper, filled with disjointed and culturally biased "facts" about American history and government. There is no room for other groups, women or people of color, to place themselves within this version of history, of what it means to be a citizen. Moreover, the process of naturalization and the test itself reinforce the notion that citizenship is something that only immigrants—foreigners, strangers, aliens—need to learn. It does not recognize citizenship as a process, but rather as an end goal that one must achieve in order to "become" American.

In addition, it does not make any attempt to relate these pieces of information to the lives of those in the process of "becoming" citizens. In fact, it has very little relevance to individuals' own experiences and does not allow them to build on their own backgrounds and talents. It does not contain within it any motivation to learn about what it means to be a citizen or how to integrate one's own life experiences into that definition of citizenship and of America. Put simply, the test is something to be memorized, regurgitated, and then quickly forgotten.

Seen in juxtaposition with this test, the telling of these stories

11. Lowe, Lisa. Immigrant Acts. Durham: Duke University Press. p. 55. 1996.

becomes all the more important. The space created by this book offers a critical alternative to "mainstream" definitions of citizenship and America. This book presents a public forum in which individuals can declare their own realities, craft their own identities, and claim the freedom to express their authentic experiences.

Knowing Something of the Old Ways...

The role of this type of public validation is essential in strengthening the individual. However, the individual does not live in a vacuum. Life stories must take into account the entirety of the individual's experience. For many people this means family. The relationship between generations is particularly important within immigrant families and communities. Often children of immigrants do not see their parents' talents and backgrounds with pride. In the US, where the dominant culture views material wealth as the measuring stick for success, the rich traditions and cultural wealth that immigrants bring to this country are not valued. Indeed, some children are even ashamed of their backgrounds, of their parents' accented English, of their own native language. They do not often see their parents' strengths publicly valued. One Hmong high school student, Nicole Ly, described the importance of public validation of her background.

> At home, I'm not interested in Hmong culture, but at Jane Addams School, I learn a lot from the people and the "Cultural Exchange." Then I often go to my mom about these things and she explains them to me. I'm interested in Hmong culture because others are interested. At home, it feels like my mom is lecturing me. In the "Cultural Exchange," others are talking. Jane Addams School has had a good effect on my life. I look at my culture in a better way. I am more proud to be Hmong. [12]

The creation of a public space in which parents can tell their stories provides an opportunity for children of immigrants to view their parents and their own backgrounds and cultures in a new light. It can make them see that while their parents may have to depend on them occasionally to navigate their new society, they also have valuable knowledge and insight to share. It can clarify for to them the struggles and strengths of their parents and help ground them as they work to create an identity that incorporates the old and the new. Kai Lee, a Hmong high school student, very eloquently describes the need for this grounding:

> It's hard enough going through life thinking about how to survive in America. It's even harder when I think about how

12. Interview with Nicole Ly, Summer, 1998.

to survive in two cultures at the same time, in America....I'm afraid that one day, we will lose everything that defines us. When that time comes, we will not quite be Americans, and we will not be Hmong either. We will be someone who is in between, who knows little of both....People will say we are Hmong, but our heart will no longer be. [13]

Capturing the stories of elders is a first step in preventing the future that Kai anticipates with fear and heartache. Seen in this light, the telling of these stories becomes all the more imperative.

Defining an Uncertain Identity

In *Writing Our Lives*, a collection of autobiographies of American Jews, editor Steven Rubin writes of the importance of telling life stories for Jewish immigrants in the US.

The immigrant experience was characterized above all by a conflict of values, by attempts to reconcile new attitudes with old customs. For the immigrant writer, autobiography offered a means of defining an uncertain identity within a new and often alien culture, a way of imposing order on experience that was often confusing and chaotic. Equally important, it provided a vehicle for linking personal history with that of the group, with an entire social process. In retelling the story of their lives, these authors re-created the collective experience of their people.[14]

The telling of life stories, then, can benefit immigrant individuals and communities in a variety of ways. First, it can serve as a means of establishing one's identity—a public proclamation of self. Second, it can link individuals to other individuals, to communities, and to larger social contexts.

Collective Autobiography?

There is a tension inherent in this linkage, however, between creating a positive community identity and reinforcing stereotypical assumptions. When a member of a dominated group speaks out, their story can come to be seen as a communal utterance, a collective tale, rather than one person's lived experience. As Henry Louis Gates, Jr. writes of slave narratives, in telling their stories individuals knew that the "character, integrity, intelligence, manners and morals of the entire community were staked on published evidence provided by one of their number."[15] We must ask what the effect of this knowledge is on the story that is told. A

13. Kai Lee, Journal, 11/23/98.
14. Rubin, Steven (ed.). Writing Our Lives: Autobiographies of American Jews. Philadelphia: The Jewish Publication Society. p. xviii 1991.
15. Padilla, Genaro. My History, Not Yours: The Formation of Mexican American Autobiography. Madison: University of Wisconsin Press. p. 8 1993.

second example comes from Carlos Bulosan's *America is in the Heart*. In the introduction to this work, Carey McWilliams writes that "it reflects the collective life experience of thousands of Filipino immigrants."[16] To us, this is a problematic statement, for how can one person write for thousands? How can one write about the experiences of people from an excluded and often unheard group and make their voices heard without them becoming representative of the entire group? Instead of reinforcing stereotypes, how can we discover the universality of human experience that enables us to form meaningful connections within and across groups?

Eliminating "Ethnic Species"

One answer to these questions is to present the life stories of a variety of people—to show the diversity of individuals through a deliberate process that recognizes the difference inherent in all of us. Public presentation of life stories has the potential to alter the way we view "Americans," a fight against both a mythological national identity and a faulty notion of multiculturalism. As our nation and our communities continue to grow increasingly diverse, this process takes on renewed importance. Unfortunately, the "mainstream" response to this growing diversity has been to "add on" a unit or a month of "diversity." In this rendering, multiculturalism is not equated with many cultures, but as cultures other than the dominant European culture. However, creating public spaces

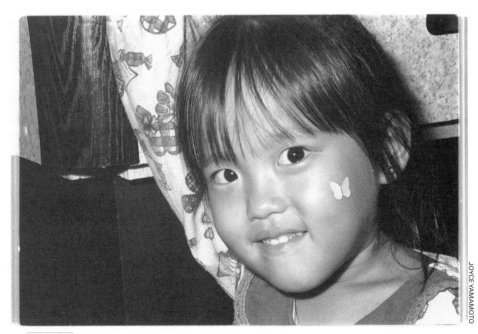

JOYCE YAMAMOTO

16. Bulosan, Carlos. America is in the Heart. Seattle: University of Washington Press. p. vii. 1973.

for the sharing of individual stories can fight against this trend. In hearing and presenting the diverse voices of individuals, multiculturalism develops a broader meaning—listening to multiple voices. It means "recognizing, valuing, and empowering every one of [us]"[17]

In addition, listening to the authentic voices of individuals in this way allows multiculturalism and diversity to signify more than racial or ethnic difference. Each of us brings our unique experiences, background and viewpoint to our lives. This is the true meaning of societal pluralism that we must convey. Diversity thus means a sharing of selves so that our personal stories and interpretations create a space for each of our unique cultural expressions.

> By inviting students to share their own stories or express their interpretations… teachers not only allow students to construct knowledge and make meaning… but also enable them to share their perspectives and cultural values.[18]

In viewing multiculturalism as the product of our unique voices and perspectives, we begin to move outside of the cultural boxes that have been constructed by traditional views of diversity. When "culture" is taught using "facts" rather than authentic voices and lived experiences, people become members of a group and not individuals. They become what Danling Fu describes as "ethnic species" rather than unique selves. Being labeled in this way denies the interplay of the many and varied forces that shape one's unique life experience. It begs the question asked by Maxine Hong Kingston, "When you try to understand what things in you are Chinese, how do you separate what is peculiar to childhood, to poverty, insanities, one family, your mother who marked your growing with stories, from what is Chinese?"[19]

By incorporating authentic voices, however, this problem can be averted; we can begin to see the complexity and subtleties within individuals. As Elaine Kim writes, "sharing life stories presents an opportunity to take apart a congealed image of ethnicity and culture."[20] It broadens our definition of culture, bringing us to see that there is no one "American culture" or "Hmong culture", but rather a continuum of cultural expressions.

We have experienced this transformation first-hand in our work at the Jane Addams School. In working with individuals, developing genuine relationships, we have come to know each other not as representatives of a culture—be it Hmong, Latino, youth, or professional culture—but as people. As Terri Wilson, a college student at the School, explained, "You must care for a person inside their culture; care for more than just learning about their culture. You must want to

17. Fu, Danling, My Trouble is My English: Asian Students and the American Dream. Westport: Boynton/Cook Publishing. p. 211. 1995.
18. Ibid., p. 212.
19. Kingston, Maxine Hong. Woman Warrior: Memoirs of a Girlhood Among Ghosts. New York: Vintage Books. p. 5. 1975.
20. Kim, Elaine H. and Yu, Eui-Young. East to America: Korean American Life Stories. New York: The New Press. p. xi. 1996.

know the person inside."[21]

We recently experienced a striking example of this shift, of people moving from an "ethnic species" framework to a personal understanding of an individual. Several college students who were unfamiliar with Hmong history and culture wanted to meet with Shao Lee, one of the Hmong women whose story is told here. The students arrived with questions in hand relating to religion and marriage ceremonies, cultural beliefs and practices, and the immigrant experience. After about thirty minutes of answering their questions, Shao turned the tables. She asked the very same questions back to the group—most of whom were European American—and a very interesting thing happened. No one wanted to answer. Everyone said, "well, it depends on the person" or "it's really different for everyone." Shao was extremely frustrated by this; she could not understand why no one would answer her.

This experience served as an excellent opportunity to reflect on the way in which we expected her to represent an entire group of people and "Hmong Culture" as if it were a monolithic, static entity for which she was a spokesperson, yet none of us was willing to do the same for "American Culture." This was a critical lesson. We were forced to question our assumptions and ask ourselves some important questions, questions we should carry in our minds at all times. Why do we realize that there is no one person who can speak for our "culture", but expect others to do just that for "theirs"? Why do we assign others to group categories, thus denying their individuality, when we would not want to do that to ourselves?

21. Interview with Terri Wilson, summer 1998.

I, Too, Sing America [22]

The public sharing of diverse voices allows us to stand in opposition to the myth of a "national identity." We can crack open the circumscribed definition of what it means to be American. In *America is in the Heart*, Carlos Bulosan reclaims the power to define America, not simply as the picture of material success and happy (white) faces, but as a land that recognizes and values the struggles of all people in their attempt to create our common world.

> It is but fair to say that America is not a land of one race or one class of men. We are all Americans that have toiled and suffered and known oppression and defeat...America is not merely a land or an institution. America is in the hearts of men that died for freedom; it is also in the eyes of men that are building a new world...America is also the nameless foreigner, the homeless refugee, the hungry boy begging for a job and the black body dangling on a tree. America is the illiterate immigrant who is ashamed that the world of books and intellectual opportunities is closed to him. We are all that nameless foreigner, that homeless refugee, that hungry boy, that illiterate immigrant and that lynched black body. All of us, from the first Adams to the last

---

22. Hughes, Langston, "I, Too." From Rampersad, Arnold (ed.), The Collected Poems of Langston Hughes. New York: Vintage Classics. 1994

Filipino, native born or alien, educated or illiterate—We are America! [23]

Thus we must, each of us, claim all the stories that comprise America, those of prosperity and those of struggle. They represent the continuum of our experiences, our national identities. The stories included here represent a similar attempt to break open an exclusive definition of culture and identity. What we present is not, however, a new "identity," but rather an intervention of sorts into the misconceived notion of any one definable, static cultural entity.

In sharing our personal struggles to become Americans, we participate in the renewal of America and our democracy. Ralph Ellison once said that "democracy is meaningful to the extent that people have struggled to achieve it." These stories, and the work they grow out of, represent in some way our efforts to (re)create democracy. The public recognition of these struggles is an important first step in refreshing American democracy.

We Are the Freedom People

This book is an important public forum in which the voices of individuals can be heard. It offers an opportunity for public validation and reflection. It introduces a means for people's struggles and experiences to be shared. The result of this sharing is powerful. For immigrants and their children it can provide an important bridge between the old and the new. It offers a place to publicly craft and declare our identities. It connects people to larger societal and historical forces and communities, while at the same time deliberately working to dismantle stereotypical preconceptions. Perhaps most importantly, by cracking open the myths of a "national identity," a circumscribed notion of citizenship, or static and definable "cultures," it can serve as an example to all of us that we, too, deserve to have our stories told. That our struggles have meaning and value. In the words of Lee Her, "We are the freedom people," and we, too, are America.

Jennifer L O'Donoghue and
D'Ann Urbaniak Lesch

---

23. Bulosan, Carlos. America is in the Heart. Seattle: University of Washington Press. p. 189. 1973.

Creating Democratic Spaces: Jane Addams School for Democracy

By Nick Longo
and John Wallace

Jane Addams School for Democracy (JAS) is a community-based education and action center located in Neighborhood House, a 100 year-old settlement house on the West Side of St. Paul. The School is a collaborative effort of Latino and Hmong families of the West Side, the College of St. Catherine, the University of Minnesota, the Center for Democracy and Citizenship at the Hubert H. Humphrey Institute, and Neighborhood House. Jane Addams School is based on an approach to learning in which everyone is seen as a contributor and a resource. The mission of Jane Addams School is to free and cultivate the talents, cultures, and interests of people from diverse backgrounds and traditions in order to add their energy and wisdom to the building of our communities.

What is the Jane Addams School for Democracy?

To begin to answer this, we invite you to accompany us, in imagination, on a walking tour of Neighborhood House on a Wednesday evening. The evening's work began at 6 PM with a reflection meeting involving high school students, college students and professors, discussing the work they have been doing in recent weeks and planning for the upcoming "learning circles" with neighborhood residents that began at 7 PM. Now, at 8 PM, when our tour begins, things are in full swing.

In the first room we find the Hmong-English Circle. There are twenty Hmong adults, five high school students, and fifteen college students distributed around the room at five seminar-type tables, talking and working, mostly one-on-one. The room is buzzing with talk and laughter. The pairs are working on exchange of languages and cultures, the Hmong adults improving their English speaking and writing skills, and the college students listening to stories and learning to speak and understand a little Hmong. Many of the Hmong adults are also learning about United States history and government, preparing to pass the citizenship examination. People are moving about, getting maps, pictures, and books from a resource table at one end of the room, and bringing them back to work on with their partners. Some of the high school and college students are bilingual in Hmong and English and they sometimes get pulled temporarily away from the pair in which they are working to provide translation assistance to a pair in which both partners are monolingual. From time to time a Hmong child, or two or three, will come into the room to check in for a few minutes with a parent, and will sometimes stay a while, to assist with translation or to show off the results of a crafts project that is going in the Children's Circle.

As we leave this room, to walk down the hall a bit to the large Youth Center room, which houses the Children's Circle, we pass a small kitchen where we see five children, a high school student and two college students crowding around the counter and the stove. They are laughing and chatting—busy preparing snacks for the Children's Circle. Tonight is pizza squares; last time it was brownies, varying from night to night as the participants decide. It is a much-prized privilege to be on the snack preparation team, a privilege that is passed around in an egalitarian spirit to all of the older children who participate in the Children's Circle, so that each gets to help prepare and serve snacks about every fourth week. Having tasted a preview sample of the snacks, thrust on us with smiles and giggles, we are now in the Youth Center where the Children's Circle is located. Tonight, sixty children, ranging in age from three to thirteen are working with twenty high school and college students. If the Hmong-English Circle was buzzing, this room is BUZZING. We see the children spread around the room in many small groups—a group making puppets; a group reading stories; a group piecing together puzzles; a group practicing a Hmong dance; a group building with legos; and so on. The high school and college students are sprinkled among the groups as coaches.

Leaving the Children's Circle, on our way to the Spanish-English Circle, we pass a lounge where there is a small group, a college student and three older children, working quietly. This is the creative writing group, children writing stories and poetry about their communities and their experiences. They have moved from the Youth Center for the peace and quiet of the lounge. Writing in progress!

We come now to the Spanish-English Circle. Normally this group would parallel the Hmong-English Circle—except a slightly smaller number, say ten Spanish speaking adults and ten high school and college students working in pairs exchanging language skills. But tonight is a special night—the Spanish-English Circle has a fair number of these—where the topic is food from different cultures and the learning method is experiential. In down to earth terms, it is a potluck dinner where each person has brought a dish that connects with his or her cultural background. What we see is people sharing a meal and having conversations in Spanish and English.

We are just about through with our tour, but not quite. As we leave the Spanish-English Circle and continue down the hall, we pass another small room where three older Hmong adults are working with a younger Hmong woman. The Hmong adults are preparing to take the United States citizenship examination, and because of circumstances having to do with a combination of their age and length of time in this country, they are able to take the examination in Hmong and do not have to demonstrate speaking ability or literacy in English.

Finally we visit another small room, where four children are working with an equal number of college students on the children's homework. The topics range across all school subjects, from English to science. The college students do not do the homework for the children but rather coach the children, ask questions, suggest other examples to think about, and so on. The atmosphere here is focused and quiet, for the most part, with gusts of relaxation, laughter, conversation around the room, then back to work.

Taking this tour on a Wednesday evening, you have seen a lot of what goes on at Jane Addams School. You have seen the multi-cultural and intergenerational character of everything that happens. You have seen the relaxed, informal atmosphere. But there is much you have missed, as is inevitable with a single visit. You missed the ad hoc planning groups that are constantly sprouting up, and you missed the special activity groups that meet on their own schedules outside the core Monday and Wednesday evening meeting times. You missed, for example, the girls' Earth Day Club and boys' Team Boyz Club, made up of girls and boys and college student coaches, which meet on Thursday afternoons. You missed the weekly field trips to a farm in Wisconsin that take place in the summer. You missed the group of Hmong women and college students who are weaving a paj ntaub quilt together. You missed the day-long Freedom Festival which participants in Jane Addams School created in a West Side park last July, and the planning meetings and rehearsals that led up to the Festival. You missed the Health and Wellness group, college students and neighborhood residents who meet on Monday evenings to discuss issues and plan activities related to health. And you missed the Public Achievement group from Humboldt High School preparing a video on the citizenship exam based on their experiences as immigrants and their work at Jane Addams School.

How did Jane Addams School come to be?

In the summer of 1996 a group of students and faculty from University of Minnesota and the College of St. Catherine, and staff from Neighborhood House in St. Paul's West Side neighborhood, began discussing issues around education and how our universities could be greater resources to the community. We wanted to end the gulf between the university and the community. We knew that people in the community had a great deal to teach, but we didn't have a way to make legitimatize their teaching.

We were all hoping to create democratic spaces that had two characteristics. First, spaces of hospitality; spaces where people felt safe and felt free to be creative and be themselves; spaces which cultivated relationships. And they should be spaces without hierarchies of authority or knowledge, where choices about what to learn and how to learn it, what to do and how to do it, would be discussed and decided on by those affected by the choice.

Those who forged this vision in the summer of 1996 knew that if it were implemented—if such safe and democratic spaces were created and people participated in them—it would be impossible to foresee what Jane Addams School would be like in two years or even in one. Our first steps included consulting various groups of West Side residents who were already participating in other Neighborhood House programs about what they wanted to learn. They wanted to work on the citizenship exam and language acquisition. And to the question, "Would you be comfortable working with college students and what could these students learn from you?" the answer was, "Yes, college students could learn from us about Hmong and Hispanic cultures." With this input from neighborhood residents, in September 1996 Jane Addams School started one learning circle, with Hmong, Spanish, and English speakers, neighborhood residents and college students, all together.

As the above account of its origins makes clear, Jane Addams School was not designed to be a place which provides a particular curriculum; rather, it is a space that engenders an open-ended set of learning opportunities.

JOYCE YAMAMOTO

These learning opportunities can grow and change through time in response to neighborhood residents' desires for learning, with the universities as constant partners in that learning. We try to form relationships, be in constant conversation with the community, and wherever the participants want to go, the School goes. This means that the School demands from its members not just their participation in existing programs, but their vision and creativity to make the School improve, adapt, and, where appropriate, expand its work.

One of the core lessons being learned at Jane Addams School is the importance of putting an emphasis on relationships. The voices of people involved with Jane Addams School sing loudly:

Relationships are the Soul of the School.

As one of the college students put it, "The most important creation of Jane Addams School has been the community of relationships that has developed among the participants." These relationships are genuine, open and reciprocal relations where presence with people and personal connections are central. Further, participants argued that to have the most impact, relationships had to be consistent and ongoing.

From our work together at Jane Addams School, we have realized that to create safe, democratic spaces, relationships must be cultivated by the structure of the School. Talking with participants in Jane Addams School has disclosed that to cultivate genuine relationships, community members and college students must be given the opportunity to develop consistent, ongoing and multidimensional relationships. Neighborhood residents, especially, were adamant about not wanting one time programs; rather, community members desire an ongoing partnership of sustained dialogue with the universities to create new knowledge and address community issues. In this type of sustained dialogue, the relationships put an emphasis on working with, rather than doing for, and allows democratic spaces to flourish. It is within these spaces that our common struggles to become ourselves and to be creators of our common world find meaning.

University of Minnesota

Twin Cities Campus

D'Ann Urbaniak Lesch
Community Program Specialist

Center for Democracy and Citizenship
Humphrey Institute of Public Affairs
130 Humphrey Center
301–19th Avenue South
Minneapolis, MN 55455

626 7690
612-625-5536
Fax: 612-625-3513
E-mail: durbaniak@hhh.umn.edu

The Hmong:
Fighting to be Free*

The Hmong are a people whose culture originated in China over 4,000 years ago. Because the Hmong had a unique culture, practicing their own customs, speaking their own language, and following their own religious beliefs, they faced centuries of persecution from the Chinese who wished to conquer them. In the 1700's, many Hmong clan leaders began to lead their people South into Northern Vietnam, Laos, and Thailand hoping to find a land where they could be free.

Wanting to maintain their own cultural traditions, the Hmong did not attempt to integrate into the majority ethnic societies of their new homelands, in the low-lying areas. They settled, therefore, into the mountainous highlands of these countries, where they practiced slash and burn agriculture. Despite their search for freedom, they continued to face discrimination and persecution from the ethnic majority groups in their new countries. In Laos, for example, the Hmong were referred to as "Meo" or "Miao", pejorative names that imply barbarism, and they were treated as second-class citizens.

When the French colonized the Kingdom of Laos in the late 1800's, many Hmong sided with the French, who tended to treat them better than the ethnic Lao. After the French left Laos in 1953, North Vietnamese and Lao Communists (the Pathet Lao) began to attack Hmong homelands. Beginning in the late 1950's, as the US entered into the Vietnam conflict, the CIA began covertly to recruit the Hmong

*Historical information comes from Jane Hamilton-Merritt, "Tragic Mountains: the Hmong, the Americans, and the Secret Wars for Laos, 1942-1992." Estimates on the numbers of Hmong currently living in the United States come from the Minneapolis Star Tribune, 10/25/98.

[23]

and provide them with weapons and training.

For twenty years, the Hmong played a critical role in the "Secret War in Laos" by holding off the Communists on the ground as well as saving numerous American pilots shot down while on bombing raids over the Ho Chi Minh Trail. When their General, Vang Pao, made the alliance with the Americans, the Hmong were promised a safe place to live if the Communists succeeded in taking over Laos, a place where they could be free.

In June 1974, the Americans withdrew from Laos, and in May of the following year, the Communists took control of the country, establishing the Lao People's Democratic Republic (LPDR or Lao PDR). Soon after this, the Lao PDR publicly announced a plan to "wipe out" the Hmong, and Communist troops began a brutal campaign to punish those who had fought against them. Men who were soldiers were killed or taken away to "reeducation camps". Entire villages of people were massacred.

Thousands of Hmong fled across the Mekong River to refugee camps in Thailand. From these camps, many Hmong have resettled in the United States, Australia, France, and French Guyana, still searching for a place where they can be free. Currently, there are around 250,000 Hmong living in the United States – the largest number outside of China (where close to 7 million Hmong still live). The Hmong population in the Twin Cities of Minneapolis and St. Paul, Minnesota is estimated to be nearly 75,000, the largest in the US.

JOYCE YAMAMOTO

"This is America. You have opportunities, you can do things here."

Mai Neng Moua

Section 1
Yer Vue Moua
After reading my
Mothers story...
Mai Neng Moua

What it means to be
Hmong

Yer Vue Moua

Ever since I was old enough, I've always worked very hard...

I don't remember how old I was, but the first thing my mother taught me was to do Paj Ntaub, to do needlework.

This was the first thing I learned.

When I was very young, I didn't really know how to do anything. But I still had to work very hard. When they fed the animals, they would assign me to watch over the pigs and chickens to make sure that other people's animals would not come to eat the food. I had to scare them away. Even if I was sleeping, my family would come and drag me by the feet, pulling me away.

"You must wake up!"

That was before I was old enough to go to the garden with my mom. Once I knew how, once I was old enough, I would go with her to the garden everyday. My mom would teach us, the young children, how to work alongside her. Sometimes, our farms were far from our house, and we would have to walk for several hours to get there. I don't know how old I was when I started to work at the farm, but I was old enough that when I wasn't tired I could farm, but if I was tired I would just sit on a rock or on a log. I knew how to find insects in the rotten trees, and I would go and dig them up.

That's how old I was.

One day, when my brother and I were alone at the farm, we were naughty, and some bees attacked us. I don't remember how it happened. All of a sudden they were all around us. They came down like rain. My brother, who was older, looked at me and said, "You don't know what to do, so I'm going to run ahead and build a fire to scare them off. You run along." This was because when you make a fire the smoke will scare them away. After all the bees had gone, we were covered in bee stings. We didn't know how to take the stingers out, so we just used a knife to scrape them off. I had stings all over my head and my back, but we just scraped them off with a knife.

We didn't know what else to do.

When I was a little older, I learned how to carry corn. My family would make me go to pick up the corn, and I would carry it in a basket on my back. I also learned to use tools to grind the corn and to remove the husk from rice. If I was at home, I had to make dinner for the entire family and also feed the pigs and chickens. This was when I was a little older.

It was very hard to make money...

It was very difficult for my family to make money. We lived several days' journey away from the market. In one whole season, our family, and we were one of the richer families, could make only ten bars of silver. That was considered a lot of money! Even so, it was only for the older kids and the boys.

Every year, I would look forward to the New Year celebration and hope that I would be able to wear all the things I had made during the year, all the beautiful things. But only the older kids would get to wear the new clothes and the silver. Being the youngest one, I would only get to wear the older stuff.

> Little ones only wore older things, old clothes.

Our money also went for education. In my family, an important family, we sent two boys to school in a town that was very far away. For one year, we paid one silver bar for each boy. My family struggled to support them. We all worked so hard, but we could hardly make enough money to cover their educational expenses.

We were only farmers, but we suffered a lot...

When the war started, they took my father away—the enemy, the Communists. We were only farmers, we didn't really know about fighting. But we suffered a lot. We were civilians, so we suffered from both sides. One side would make us help them, and then the other side would come and make us help them, too. When the French officials or soldiers came to our region, they would stay with my family. When the Communists came, they would also stay with my family. But they were fighting each other, so they would both say,

> "You are feeding the enemy."

This caused many problems.

My father was an official, like a village judge; whenever people had disputes, they would come to him, and he would decide how to settle their claims. He was in charge of our whole region. Eventually, the French gave my father a special government stamp. This caused people in the region to be jealous, both the Hmong people and the Communists. Some of these jealous Hmong people went to the Communists and told them that my family was working for the French.

That's when they came and took my father away.

My family had gone together to work at the farm. My parents needed to go back to our house—they were going to go home for one night and come back the next day—but we, the children, stayed at the farm. On their way home, my father was captured by the Communist soldiers. My parents didn't come back. We were alone at the farm for ten days, my brother and me. We had some chickens at the farm, and we had to guard them.

That's why we stayed there.

When they took my father away, they beat him very badly. They broke his hip. The French went to get him and brought him back to their camp to heal him. At that time, all my brothers took up arms. We decided to be on just one side, to take a position. The Communists had forced us to do this. They had taken my father away and hurt him. After my family made this decision, we were no longer afraid.

We were on one side.

When the Communists learned that we had taken up arms, they came and burned all our crops. They burned all the rice at the farm. And so the French had to give us rice; they made rice drops.

From that point on, we were in the war, always fighting...

After the French left, the Americans came to stay with us, with the Hmong people. I don't understand why, but the Communists hated the Americans even more than the French. As a result, every time the Americans came to stay with us, we would have to move—every three months.

We couldn't live in our own homes anymore.

We stayed in camps. Every few months our camp would be broken up. The Communists were always fighting us, so only the soldiers would stay. The rest of us would run to another place, another village or the military base.

There were only two Americans. All that for only two Americans! Not twenty or a whole troop, just two. If a lot of Americans had come, then we could have won the war!

But there were only two.

The Communists really hated these two Americans. They believed, "Oh the Americans are in that military base", so they came to destroy us. The Communists called us the hands and feet of their enemies, the Americans. The Communists were always telling us, "Don't be on their side, don't let them come live with you. They're only here to destroy your country. They're only here to divide the people." But we didn't believe them.

We knew we could not go and live with the Communists. When the Communists were threatening to hurt us, we would run and hide in the forests. When we returned, they would have taken the wings, the heads, and the legs of our little chickens and wrapped them all together and left them on our stoves as a symbol that they wanted to do the same things to us; they wanted to kill our families in the same way.

We could not live safely with them.

So even if there were only one or two Americans with us, the Communists came and attacked our base, and then we would run away. We couldn't stay there anymore. Only the men would stay in the military base, all the women, the wives of the soldiers, would stay in other villages. When there was a lot of fighting and we lost the base, then we would run away with the men.

The Americans couldn't run at all! I remember once when we were running from the military base, one American came out of the base and he lost his shoes! I don't know how old I was, but I had to take off my apron and wrap it around his feet. My brother and I had to take the American, one of us on each side, and help him run.

Oh! He was a big guy!

It was raining, and we were all wet. It rained all day and all night for seven days. We ran and ran. My brother and I didn't have any shoes either. It was slippery, and there were thorns and stones in the road, but we didn't feel anything. We were so afraid. We ran to a place where a helicopter could come to get him. It did, and we never knew what happened to him. They came and took him away. We went back to the base.

The other American had died at the base. Later, the Americans came and dug up his body and took him away too.

Because of the war we could only farm a little bit, so they would have to drop off rice for us. It was like this for many years, from the time the war started with the French, all the way through the time we had to come to America.

Soon the whole village ran...

When the Americans left, General Vang Pao left. He left all his soldiers in Laos. My husband was a soldier, and all my brothers too. But after the Americans had left, the Communists started to take people away.

Each person one by one.

In the beginning, they said they were just going to "reeducate" them. First they would take them to a house in town. They would let them stay there while they taught them. Then, they started to take them away in helicopters to a town far away. Everyone knew that if they went in the helicopter, they would never return.

So they ran away.

JOYCE YAMAMOTO

When all the husbands had run away, the Communists started coming after the wives. The wives began to run, and soon the whole village ran! We ran and hid in the mountains and the jungles. We joined the Chao Fa, the guerilla fighters, to fight, to survive.

We couldn't live like this...

We hid in the jungles and fought from them. Every one of us had to carry a gun. My husband and I had three guns—even I had one! The Communists wanted to confiscate all the guns, so we had to hide them.

We lived in the jungles for about three years. That's when my husband died, when we were fighting in the jungle.

When we were in the jungle, we had to struggle to find food. At that time we had no markets, no way to get food. We tried to farm, but the Communists made it impossible for us. They would come three times. In the beginning of the season, they came so that we couldn't clear the land. The second time was when we tried to plant the rice. The third time was when the rice was ready to be harvested.

They would burn the rice.

The Communist soldiers would also come and stay in any places where there was food. At night we had to take a couple of guerilla soldiers to go with us and steal the rice, our rice. In the jungles, we had to rely on leaves and tubers. We would eat a vegetable similar to a potato or a yam. When we had a little bit of food, we would be very conservative in what we ate to make sure that we had enough.

To make sure that it would last a long time.

That was the time that my parents died. They died from hunger. Most of the young children died too, even though their parents worked hard to find food for them to eat. We were hungry, very hungry. Because my husband died during that time, I had to work even harder to find food for my three little children. They were so young, so little, that they couldn't really help me at all. We couldn't live like this. We couldn't stay there any longer.

We had to find a way to get to Thailand.

We didn't think we would ever come to this country...

We tried three times before we made it to Thailand. I had three very small children and my husband and parents had died already, so it was very difficult for me. We lost everything on our journey through the mountains, through the jungles, and across the Mekong River. When we finally arrived in Thailand, all we had left were the clothes we were wearing. We had to beg from other people for everything, for food, for a few articles of clothing.

In Thailand I went to find work. For a whole day of work, I was paid only ten Baht [around 35 cents]. I knew that if we lived in Thailand, there would be no one to help us. We could not survive on only ten Baht a day.

I decided to start the paperwork to go to America. When we had crossed the Mekong River to Thailand I had lost all our papers, so the American man at the refugee camp did the paperwork for us. We didn't know what year we were born, so the American would look at us and from our size determine how old we were.

> He made up our birthdays.

We waited one year after all the paperwork, and then we came to the United States. We didn't think we would ever come to this country, but we had no choice. Even in this country, everything was so dark.

> It was like we lived in darkness.

We didn't know if it was safe here. At night we would take all the tables and all the chairs and put them up against the door. My children were so afraid, so we all huddled together and nobody wanted to be on the outside. They would cry if they had to be on the outside.

We came here to find freedom...

Life in this country is very different from our life in Laos. We came here to find freedom, but in this country there are many different ways to be free as well as many ways not to be. One way that we are free is that we can go to school, even if we are old. One thing I understand is that if there had been no war, then we might not have had education like this. This country has helped me to see further, to see far and wide. I have been able to see how people in this country live, what their lives are like. I am able to see how far along everyone else is, but also how far behind I am. Seeing this, I start running after them. But I am very old now.

> Maybe I will never be able to catch them.

If I had had education like this when I was younger, maybe we wouldn't have to live in public housing now. My family never had to beg for food before we left Laos. We never had to work for other people. There were always people who came to work for us. There were always people who came to ask us for food.

But now we've lost all this. Here we have to beg for food. We have lost because now we have to work for other people. We have to ask other people for assistance. I have lost.

We lost our country...

One of the things that is most upsetting to me is that we lost our country. We lost people whom we loved. We lost our homeland. We lost everything that we couldn't carry with us in our hands when we ran away. If it weren't for the war and the fighting we would have had freedom in Laos. But we were not free because the Communist soldiers attacked us.

> If not for all that, we would have been free in our country.

The farms, the forests, the trees, they were all ours. Whatever tree you wanted to cut was yours to cut. I heard a rumor that the Communists are cutting down our trees now. I am just afraid that when all the young Hmong people go back to Laos, there won't be any trees for them to see. They have paved all the roads to our towns and old villages already. I have heard that now people come one day and just tie a rope around a tree and the next day it will be gone, taken away. It hurts me very much. It hurts my heart that all that we had is gone now. Our relatives are dead.

> Now they've even taken the trees from us.

Our life before seems like it was just a dream. The life when we had our own house, our own food, and our own animals, that is in the past. Now it is gone.

I don't think I'll ever see freedom...

We lost so much in coming to this country, and in many ways we don't even have the freedom we came to find. One of the ways that we are not free is that we cannot speak for ourselves. I can go to school, but I don't know all the words. I can speak a little English, but I don't understand everything.

When I go to the hospital or the doctor, I have to ask someone to translate for me. It makes me upset that if I had to call the police to come to my house, I could not even talk to them. Even if I ask someone to come and translate for me, I don't know if they'll really say

[34]

what I want them to say.

The welfare reform cuts represent another way we are not free in the United States. Every day the government talks about how they are going to cut all the Asians from assistance. They say if you're not a citizen, you can not get assistance. It reminds me of the beginning of the war in Laos. It's not like people are using guns to fight, but it is the same as a war. These are the sounds of war.

The voices of war.

Before, in our own country, we were at the top. We controlled our own lives. But in this country, we are always under someone. We don't belong in that position. I just keep thinking, "This is your life now. This is your life." At this age I don't think I'll ever see freedom. I don't think I'll ever see that. My life will always be hard. Other people who have all the things here—a job, a place to live—they have freedom.

For me there is no freedom.

So many things I want my children to learn from me...

I always try to teach my children about the Hmong culture. I try to teach them how we farmed in Laos. I teach them that there is a certain time you should plant each vegetable. They need to know when to plant the corn, the sugarcane, the bananas, and the pineapples. This is important so that they can grow these plants.

If they know, they will always have food to eat.

I teach them what I have learned from farming in both Laos and in America. Now that I think about it, maybe we didn't know as much in Laos. For example, the riverbanks would have been perfect for planting. But we didn't have to worry about that there. Whenever we found a piece of land, the soil was always good for whatever we would plant, and we could reap the harvest. In Thailand, and in this country too, the soil was not as good or as rich with nutrients, so we had to put fertilizer on the soil.

If we had known about those fertilizers, we would have had even more in Laos. We didn't use fertilizers in Laos. We just planted wherever we wanted, and we always got food.

Of course that was before the war.

There were fruit trees and lots of food, so much that we couldn't even

eat it all. Our country was very good. We had all the crops and fruit, and the soil was very good. But we were so far away from the town. There was no market, no place to take it to sell. And so you would grow things to support your own family.

I could support my own family then.

There are so many things I want my children to learn from me, but they don't want to. The most important thing is how to be a family and how to farm so that you always have food to eat. If they don't learn when I'm alive, I don't know what they'll do when I'm dead. I don't know if they'll know where to put the seeds so they can have vegetables.

Another important thing is to learn what herbal medicines to use, but the children are not interested. The children think that the herbal medicine is not good, they all go to the doctor now. For me, myself, I think that the doctor is important, but the herbal medicines are too. They are just as important.

If they're not going to learn, then when I die I will take it all with me. All of my knowledge, my experience will be gone.

Then who will know about this?

I'm going to run until I get there...

I want to be a citizen here. Although I'm old, I still want it. Some people say Americans are very mean people, but I know that if the Americans had not reached out their hands to help me, I would never have been able to get here.

In this country, even if you are old, even if you can not do anything at all, you should try to get your citizenship. I am old and my life has been difficult. I have struggled through Laos and Thailand just to get here. When I got here, they said I should become a citizen, so I have struggled to do it.

The Jane Addams School has helped me in this struggle. It is different from other schools because we have time in the beginning to talk to one another. We have discussions. At other schools I have gone to, I never even had an opportunity to talk. I just listened to the teacher talk to me. The Jane Addams School is very different from those places. It's fun! I truly enjoy the times when we talk about freedom, culture, what it means to be a citizen.

I have a chance to talk.

One night at Jane Addams School there was an American girl, a college student, who asked us why we are so concerned about the citizenship test.

Why do we care so much?

Why are we working so hard?

What's the big deal?

And we thought, "Why is she even asking us these questions?" We think it's the least we can do to become part of this country.

And we really want to do it.

After reading my
mother's story…

Mai Neng Moua

There were a lot of little things that really struck me in my mom's story. For example, things about her childhood, how she had to learn how to do things at such an early age. Some of the things were really funny, but it made me think. She had such responsibilities, even as a little kid.

"Wow, she had to grow up really fast."

It also occurred to me that my mom is so politically aware. When she was talking about the trees, on one level it was about trees, but it was also about so much more. She used that as an example of how things happen in the world, of what's happening in the country.

"This is all we have and they're even taking this away from us."

She was so aware of her own position, of where she is in relation to other people, where she was before, and where she is now. And aware of how things have changed for the Hmong people—before we had our homeland, we had all of our people together, and now we don't have that. She understood that yes, we have freedom, but it's not complete freedom because we can't do this and we can't do that.

I think we younger Hmong often have this bias that now that we're in this country the parents and older people don't know what's going on. We think they're clueless about what's happening. But really that's an unfair assumption. And parents will say that too.

> "Just because you know how to read and write you think you're so smart. You think you know everything."

And we do! We have this incredible ignorance and arrogance about us, thinking that they really don't know anything now because they can't read and write. And it's just not true. They have so much world experience—life experience—that we don't have. My mom tells us this often.

> "Nej paub lus, paub ntawv, tab sim nej tsis paub txog lub neej."*

And it's true. So it was good for me to hear my mom's story.
My mom didn't really talk about the exodus story—leaving Laos for Thailand and the U.S.—so much. That's interesting because I think many people—Hmong and non-Hmong—are too focused on the exodus story, too focused on the war period. It is so extreme, so dramatic, that it sticks out in their minds. But I almost get tired of hearing that—it's too much. What I really want to hear about is what happened before the war, what life was like.

> "Yes there was war going on, but there was still life. You still loved and lived and laughed and farmed, right?"

Both Hmong and non-Hmong people are so stuck on the war piece and all the death and dying that they don't really ever focus on the other parts. So it was interesting to hear what my mom said about her life before the war. We don't usually get to hear that.

---

* "You know the language, know how to read and write, but you don't know about life. "

Mai Neng Moua

My mom often says she feels like we don't want to learn from her. This upsets me.

> "That's not true. We want to learn from you; we just have to find the time."

The way we learn about Hmong culture has changed. Before, in Laos or in Thailand, parents didn't really have to make a point of teaching us.

> "Hey, this is how you 'ua paj ntaub'*—first, you thread the needle and then you make a knot. Then to make the little square you do this."

---

* Literally, "do flower cloth." Paj Ntaub is the traditional Hmong needlework.

Back then, we sat alongside of our moms or aunts or grandmas and we just did it. This is how our parents learned, so now they don't understand why we don't know these things.

"You should know how to do this."

That's how it was in Laos. All the kids just knew it. They never had to be taught; they just did it with their parents. It was a part of them, of their everyday life.

In the U.S. there are so many distractions, so many things competing for our attention. I mean I speak English 99% of my time! And it's hard for us to know what's really important about "Hmongness." It's hard to know what are the aspects of Hmong culture that we should learn about, what we should keep. Not all things about Hmong people and Hmong culture are positive—not for me as a woman. So parents need to learn how to teach their kids what's important to know, what's important to keep. But they're not used to teaching kids how to do that. They need to learn how to make a specific point of teaching us.

"Ok, this is what this is, this is what it means, and this is how you do it."

There's never that kind of dialogue because we don't do a lot of similar activities. I know the effort has to come from both sides. I know the elders are waiting for us to go and ask them to teach us.

"Mom, what's this? What does that do?"

But they also have to tell us what we need to learn, what is a part of Hmong culture. My mom's gotten better at that because we've had fights about it.

"Why don't you know this? How old are you? Some day you're going to be a mother. Why don't you know this?"

"I don't know why I don't know this!"

Another difficulty is that now people have enough money to buy things, so we don't have to make them anymore—we just buy them. Other people make them. In the past, in Laos, people really didn't have money; they bartered or they made things themselves. There are many changes that affect the culture and how we learn about it, how we live it.

□

When my donor*, Eric, got married last year, my mom and I wanted to make him a Hmong outfit. Well, he was too tall to wear the paj ntaub that

---

* In the summer of 1997, Mai Neng had a kidney transplant. A good friend volunteered to donate his kidney to her.

we had made before. It wasn't long enough for him, so we had to extend it. My mom wanted me to do it. It was really hard. I had never done that kind of stitching before. All I did in junior high was cross-stitching. But this was a different kind of needlework, and I had never done it before. It was really difficult for me, and I got so frustrated.

> "Come on, I'm a college graduate, I can do this! This can't be that hard. I can do it. I can figure it out!"

I tried, but you can definitely see where she ended and I started. My mom was mad.

The big problem was the shirt. My mom cut the pants, which were pretty easy to sew; I could do that. But the shirt – there was no pattern. I only had a big piece of black material and this shirt that we had bought from a Hmong woman. So we measured how big he was, how long his arms were, and that was all I had to go on. I had this shirt to look at and this mess of black material.

> "Oh my god! How do you do this??"

And she got really mad at me. We got into a huge fight.

> "WHY DON'T YOU KNOW THIS?"

> "Because you never taught me. Because I've never done this before in my life. Mom, how many Hmong kids my age do you think can do this? It's not like I'm the only one who can't! I'm trying. You really need to say, 'you should learn this.'"

> "WELL YOU'D BETTER COME OVER HERE AND LEARN THIS SO THAT YOU CAN'T BLAME ME ANYMORE—SO YOU CAN'T SAY THAT I DIDN'T TEACH YOU"

Since then, she's been better at teaching me.

□

There are other things that our parents know because they grew up with them that we don't or can't just know. I videotaped an "ua neeb"* ceremony this past weekend for my mediation class, and I can see that I need to ask my mom some questions.

> "Why did people bow to the shaman before he did his ritual? Are they bowing to show their appreciation or what? What's the significance of that?"

Before they did the ceremony, they had the sick person sit on a bench

---

* An "ua neeb" is a shamanic ceremony performed in times of illness or at the New Year.

with a live pig behind her. They took a string and tied the pig to the person. After the shaman said some things, they took the pig to be butchered and then brought back it's body. I think I know why they did that. Maybe it's to tie the soul of the pig to the person so that the pig will act as a guard. If the soul loses its way, then the pig will bring the soul of the person back to their body.

This is my understanding, my interpretation, but if our parents don't explain it, it has no meaning to me. I don't understand the significance of it, and I can't explain it to other people. I don't really know. I could come up with something, but these are the kinds of things that I want and need to learn.

Not many young people actually participate in that kind of ritual anymore. We don't know what's going on, what to do. My family doesn't do these rituals anymore because we're Christian, but I still want to know what it is even if I don't do it myself. I want to understand why people do things, what the significance is. But if you don't take an interest in it, if you don't seek it out, if you're a Christian Hmong, you'll never have to run across that. If your relatives are Christian, you just hang out with that group of people and you never have to know it, hear it, see it.

□

My family became Christian when we came to the United States. We lived in a small Hmong community in Pittsburgh. About half the community went to church and the other half didn't. For my mom, as a widow, it was hard to keep up with all the Hmong traditions. The Hmong rituals are really expensive, and she didn't want to do them anymore. When someone gets sick, you have to do it. Every New Year you have to do it. You have to have money to do all those rituals—they're not cheap. So I think at first it was more economical for her to become Christian. She has a different feeling about Christianity now. Maybe at first it was just for convenience, but it has become much more than just that.

There's a lot of tension between Christian and non-Christian Hmong. There's a feeling that because you've converted to Christianity you're not as Hmong. I'm not sure how it is in American churches nowadays, but in Hmong churches we always talk about spirits. And spirits are very real to Hmong people—good spirits and bad spirits, people who've passed away, ancestors. At church, we say that a long time ago we used to believe in other spirits, but now God is our spirit. So there is a connection to the past, except you can't have both spirits because they're not alike. You have to choose one or the other, and this causes tension.

> "You're not really Hmong anymore because you don't honor
> the ancestors. You're not animist anymore. You've sold out."

This past weekend my uncle, who's not Christian, had a "noj mov" to do a "hu plig" ceremony because he had a baby*. There was a man from our church there, but he had to leave early to go to another "noj mov" for another child. It was a Christian one, and he had to go because he's the deacon that watches over that group of families. He needed to be there, but my uncle was upset.

> "Oh, you're just going to go and be with your Christian friends. You're leaving us, your family, to go and be with other people, those Christians."

He was sort of teasing, but underneath he was serious. His statement holds within it questions about the importance of the family, extended family, and the clan. The church becomes a substitution for the clan. The congregation does things that the clan would do—helping with funerals, marriages, births, and things like that. This causes more tension.

◻

I grew up going to church, being a Christian. It has become part of my life. I really can't imagine being anything else. I want my kids to go to church and believe in God. Even if they don't believe in God, they would get some good moral teachings—being good to your neighbors, respecting your parents, that kind of stuff.

Christianity is a part of my life that I'm not willing to give up when I get married. I'm not going to marry a non-Christian. It's too much to ask.

> "Ok, first you ask me to move somewhere else, to leave my family, leave my friends, my job, the place I know, all this stuff, for you, and then you ask me to give up my soul, my spirit. NO! It's too much to ask."

No, I'm not going to do that. If you're a Christian woman and you marry a non-Christian Hmong man, then you are the one who has to change, to give up your beliefs. I've never seen any of the Christian women who've married non-Christian men come back to church.

You really have to make a decision about it before you marry. Maybe you can't control who you fall in love with, maybe you can, but you have to make your choices and decide what's really important for you. What are you willing to compromise on? Sure, maybe a different state, a different job. But sometimes you can't compromise.

> "No, this is really important and if I don't have this I'm sorry, I can't marry you. You're just not the right partner for me."

◻

---

* Literally "eat rice," a "noj mov" is a party. A "hu plig," or "soul-calling" ceremony is performed to "tie" a baby's soul to its family. Traditionally performed on the third day after birth, the "hu plig" also serves as a naming ceremony.

I would define myself as a new American. Ethnically, racially, I'm still Hmong, but I say new American because I am invested in this life here in America. I will be here the rest of my life and so will my kids.

New American.

American in terms of believing in the ideals of choice, freedom and democracy, being a participant in American life, contributing what I can to it. I see myself as a part of the American life. And maybe I'm a new part, but I'm definitely an integral and connected, interconnected, part of the rest of American life.

We need to think about what this means to all of us. What is America? Who are Americans? America is in the making. It isn't a complete picture and whoever comes adds to it.

Some people say America is the melting pot, but I don't like that analogy because I'd still like to be Hmong. Maybe it's just the Midwest, but people here seem to have problems with my being Hmong or Hmong-American.

> "Why can't you just be American? My ancestors are form ireland and I don't say I'm Irish American. I'm just American. Why can't you be American?"

> "Ok, I am American, I want to be American. But do you really accept me?"

On the one hand, they say they want me to be American. Well, fine, I'm American now. But then they don't accept me as an American anyway. They'll always ask questions.

> "Where are you from?"

> "Oh, you know, Pittsburgh."

> "Well where are your parents from?"

> "Oh, they're from China."

> "Oh, OK."

And then it's like this realization for them—"Oh! That's what you are. You're really Chinese. Now I can fit you into my perception of what you are."

□

It's hard for me to say what part of me is Hmong, what part American. It's all so blended. But the most important thing to me is family. My family includes more than just my nuclear family. It includes my extended family—all my aunts and uncles and their kids and people I don't even know. The connection with family has become more and more important as I've grown up. And with the community. That's really strong for me. Wherever I am, I want to be close to the Hmong community. At least I want to know where they are, where I can get good food! Things like that.

Those are the parts of my life that I would say are more Hmong than American. Most Americans seem to have very different ideas about who's in their family. They're very nuclear family oriented. There's not as strong a sense of connection with the broader community. Community is only their friends.

☐

I tell people that I don't really represent the Hmong community because I'm on the edges of it, the fringes. My family is on the fringes mostly because my mom is a widow. She's not in the loop. She doesn't get invited to family meetings because she's not a man. Sometimes she gets so angry because she feels like the family only calls when they want money. She says that if they didn't need money, we might never hear from them. My brother is now being called in to these meetings because he's getting older; he's a man now.

I think I'm on the fringes because I'm an anomaly. I'm a twenty-four or twenty-five-year-old, unmarried, graduate student. That's really rare for a Hmong woman. So a lot of people see me as on the outside of the community. Also, I'm loud. I say what I feel, and some Hmong people don't like that. They expect girls to be quiet, not to speak up. But I'm not like that.

But even though I'm on the fringes of the community, I still feel a deep sense of responsibility towards the Hmong community. I'm getting all this education because I want to have the skills to help my community. It's hard though, because I know I will have to struggle to be accepted, especially as an unmarried woman.

☐

If I became a great sociologist and taught in a great school, I would not have as much respect in the Hmong community as I would if I were married—someone's wife, Mrs. "So and So." Maybe that's changing with this new generation, but I will never be a leader for the Hmong community as a whole. I could probably be a leader for Hmong women, but it would be hard for Hmong men to accept me. I don't think it could happen. Being politically correct, they might say that they would, but in their hearts, they would never accept it. But that's just too bad for them!

I asked my uncle about interracial marriages recently, and he put it in terms of the self versus the community.

"Do you want to help yourself or do you want to help your

community? If you marry someone who's not Hmong, then you're helping yourself; you're being selfish. If you really want to help your community, help the Hmong people, then you need to marry a Hmong man."

He's partly right, because if you marry outside of the community, it will take you twice as long and you'll have to work twice as hard to gain the trust of the community. Whereas if you marry within the Hmong culture, you already have that inside track and you don't need to work as hard. There's a stereotype too that if you marry "outside," you don't want to help Hmong people.

But if I want to help them and they don't accept my help then is it really my fault or theirs? It's time for us to change our idea of leadership. Maybe in the old days the leaders were people like General Vang Pao—men who took up arms and fought the war. But we're in a new country now and we need different kinds of arms besides guns. We need education. We need to arm ourselves with education. We need to arm ourselves with communication skills. And if you're a woman and you can help the Hmong community because you have these skills, then that's even better. We need to get away from the days of people saying,

"I'm a man and you're not being respectful to me."

That kind of thinking makes me frustrated. Some men get really pissed at me when I complain about the sexism in the Hmong community, especially men my age.

"THAT'S NOT TRUE, HOW CAN YOU BE LIKE THAT, HOW CAN YOU SAY THAT?"

"Look, try to understand. We live in a patriarchal society. You guys aren't in positions of power yet because you're not married, but people who are older, who are in positions of power, this is how they feel, how they act."

☐

Recently, in the newspaper, a Hmong leader basically stated that Hmong women are responsible for all the problems in the community. He said that for too long we've been blaming Hmong men for our difficulties, and now it's time to blame Hmong women.

This is a typical response in the community. And it's too bad because we should be asking questions about why there are problems. It's not about finding someone to blame. Maybe there are things going on that we need to look at, to investigate.

☐

My work at Jane Addams School is important because of who I am—older, educated and single. I need to be there for the young people. It's important for them to physically see somebody who is older and not married, somebody who is educated. If they just hear about something, but never see the flesh and blood of it, it's not real to them.

I wish there were more Hmong college students doing this, just being out there for the little kids to see, to know. We can help them to see that it's ok to go to school, it's ok to be single, and you don't have to get married if you don't want to. There are alternatives. There are many kinds of lives. The sad part is that if kids don't even know what the options are, then they only know one way of life. Once you can see the options, you can choose. But you can't choose when you don't even know what's out there.

I have really enjoyed working with the young girls in the Creative Writing group at Jane Addams School. I am hoping to teach them to value themselves and their opinions. I want them to see that what they want is important. I don't know how much they get of that in their own homes. It's a challenge – how do we empower these girls to become powerful women who believe in themselves and believe in their own voices?

The concept of what a good Hmong girl is needs to be talked about, discussed. Typically, for Hmong families, a good Hmong girl is one who doesn't speak up, who is quiet and polite. A good girl gets married, has kids, obeys her husband and her father and does the household work.

It's not that those things are not important. They are important, and Hmong girls are learning to do those things, but what they need to learn in addition to that is to believe in themselves and their opinions. They need to be taught to listen to what they want and to honor themselves and those wishes.

□

At a young age, especially in junior high, girls start thinking about men and how you have to have a man. They get asked "the" questions.

"Do you have a boyfriend?"

"No."

"Are you married?"

"No."

"Well, what's wrong with you??"

They are taught to think of themselves in terms of men. That's how it is for Hmong women. You're always someone's wife; you're always someone's daughter-in-law. You're the daughter of somebody, the mother of somebody. Hmong women don't have an identity until they're married. When they're single, their family is preparing for them to leave. This is true for me, too.

❑

Even though there is such a strong emphasis on marriage and having children, sometimes I get mixed signals about it from Hmong women.

> "ARE YOU MARRIED?"

> "No, I'm still a student."

> "OH GOOD! DON'T GET MARRIED!"

> "Well, what's wrong with being married??"

> "OH, OH, JUST FO TO SCHOOL AND FINISH THAT FIRST, AND DON'T GET MARRIED…"

They act like marriage is the most awful thing, like it's something evil. But you have to take that in light of what they've been through, too. In their experience, once you are married and have kids, then you cannot go to school, go to work or do the things that you want to do. They try to tell me to do the things that I want to do, and then get married. So I get these mixed signals. Some people say I'm too old, I should be married. But then other people will tell me not to get married yet, to go to school. It's so confusing!

> "What do you want me to do?? Be married, not be married? What??"

Now that my two best friends are married and one of them has a child, the pressure to get married seems greater. But I really don't care. I don't feel like it. Besides, I've never really met the right person. And everyone wants me to marry a Hmong person, and, I don't know about that. My mom and I have debates about this all the time, and we always come to the same conclusion.

> "DON'T MARRY AN AMERICAN, HE'LL JUST DIVORCE YOU. HE'LL NEVER LOVE YOU."

> "Mom, Hmong people get divorces too, right?"

> "YEAY, THAT'S TRUE."

> "You know mom, Hmong men aren't all that great."

> "YOU'RE RIGHT, THEY'RE NOT THAT GREAT EITHER."

> "Oh, man…" "OH, MAN…"

When my father died, my mom was young enough to get remarried, but she never did. I'm sad for her now. My brothers and I have our own busy lives, and I wish she had someone to take care of her. I've asked her why she never remarried, and she said the people that she wanted to marry, did not want to marry her because she had children. And she didn't want to marry the men that wanted to marry her because they were widowers with their own kids. She didn't want to have to take care of somebody else's kids. She also said that if she remarried she would not have been able to keep us. She probably would have kept me, the girl, and not my brothers.

Traditionally, when a widow remarries outside the clan, her husband's clan, she really doesn't get anything. She does not get to keep her kids, especially if they're boys. The boys always belong to the father's family. The girls maybe, if they're young. It depends on how strict the family is, too. She gets whatever she came to the marriage with. The few little things she had. She doesn't get any money. In fact, the new husband has to pay money to the family for her. But it's less this time; she's not worth as much as a single woman is.

So my mom knew that if she remarried, she probably would not have been able to keep us. We would have been left to my grandparents, who probably would not have taken care of us as well. We would have been considered orphans who lived in the family. And orphans are treated pretty rough, pretty horribly. They don't have parents, a mom and dad to give them clothes and food.

If she had been allowed to take us with her, her new husband wouldn't have loved us as much because we weren't his kids. There is that kind of discrimination. So I think she decided to be by herself. Under the circumstances, what were her choices?

But her decision to stay single is really amazing because of the emphasis in the Hmong community on marriage. Most Hmong women who lost their husbands have remarried.

□

My mom has always stayed with my father's side of the family. We visit my mom's side of the family, but we've never lived with them. Most of my mom's family is gone now. Her parents passed away in the war. They were old, and the diet was really harsh in the jungle. They were hungry; a lot of people were hungry. And like my mom has said, you really had to work hard to stay alive. If parents didn't work hard, their children died from malnutrition. So I think my grandparents were old and sick. They didn't have enough to eat, so they died.

I can see why that period is so strong in the hearts of Hmong people because it really was a traumatic time. It was hard. It has affected people a great deal. All the people who are supposed to take care of my family, my brothers and me, have died because of the war, because of being hungry. My mom had all these great brothers that got killed in the war. Only one of her brothers survived. Her youngest brother was just a young man, unmarried. The last time she saw him was when he went up in a helicopter to go to war. There's a picture that was taken of him right before he got on the helicopter. He's standing there in his uniform, holding his gun, with the helicopter behind him. That was the last time she ever saw him. My mom still has that picture.

□

I think I'm really different from kids who were born in America. I have my own set of problems and challenges because I was six when we came here. I still have memories from the war. I'm first generation Hmong-American. I don't represent all the Hmong kids in the population. I'm at a different stage.

Kids nowadays have their own set of issues that I can't quite understand. I don't understand this lack of enthusiasm about school! It's a foreign concept to me. And the kids I grew up with would probably agree with me. We were all pretty driven in school.

> "We have to do well for our families. Our families are so poor, and it's up to us. We need to do this. Not for ourselves, but for our community."

In Laos, and for people my parents age, education was a big deal. My mom didn't get to go to school, only her brothers went. They couldn't afford to send all the kids to school. People were so proud of those who were educated. They were like the kings and queens. They could read and write. Here in America we take it for granted. It's free. We don't have to pay anything, and we don't value education or teachers as much. In Laos, if the village could send just one kid to school, that was a big accomplishment. There was one person connected to the outside world. Maybe it's just the more we have, the less we appreciate it. I don't know.

Kids today don't really have that kind of pressure, that kind of drive. I don't really even know how to explain it. There are so many dynamics to consider. Some Hmong kids nowadays still can't read or write even though they were born and grew up here. Somehow they just get lost.

Even kids like my little brother. He doesn't have that same drive. He doesn't believe in education. It's really interesting because he sees the world as hopeless. It's a dark world for him. Things aren't possible. That is so different from how I see the world. I see more possibilities. I'm more hopeful.

> "This is America. You have opportunities, you can do things here."

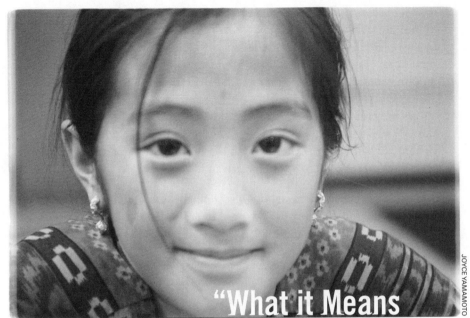

"What it Means to be Hmong"

A Collaborative Poem
by the Jane Addams School
Creative Writing Group

Laos
Warm
Live in straw house
Old house in Laos
Hmong boys are mean

Show respect
By
Hmong religion
Spirits

Rich
Respect language
Culture
Hmong clothes

Mai Moua is so tall is OK
Some Hmong are little too
We have black hair
Hmong people have long hair

Mountaintops
War
Bravery
Survival

We know how to weave
Design
Paj Ntaub
Into
Hmong dress

We wear silver earrings
Jewelry that is silver
Gold and silver

Hmong people eat chicken a lot
Rice
Purple sticky rice
We eat sticky rice with pepper sauce
Spices
Papaya salad
We eat mouse in Laos and Thailand

Hmong weddings
Beg
Beer
Men eat first
Big family lives in America

A lot of Hmong people
Different names
We all like each other very much

Thailand
Farmers
Plant Zaub Paj [flower vegetable]

Refugee camps
Thailand house
Refugees
Only one bed to sleep

America
Different

America to live

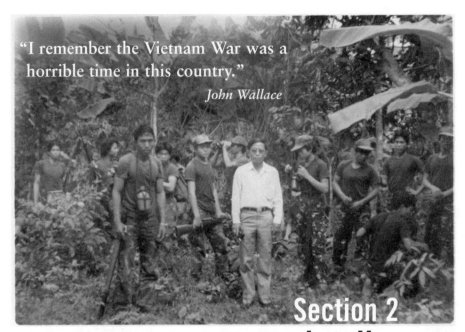

"I remember the Vietnam War was a horrible time in this country."

John Wallace

Section 2
Lee Her

Recollections of the Vietnam War Period

PETER LEACH

Lee Her

Many years ago,

when I was a boy, I lived with my family in Laos. When the Vietnam War started in 1961, I was 14 years old. I became a soldier. My father and my brother were soldiers, too. Our family had three soldiers.

A small country like Laos must use all boys and men as soldiers.

Before the war started I had gone to school. My father and other men in the village built the school with wood from the forest. At school I learned to read and write the Lao language. I learned the Lao alphabet, which has 27 letters. I learned numbers, and I learned to add and subtract. I had a chance to study history and geography. I lived in the mountains, and our teacher had to come from the valley to the mountains to teach in the school. I liked school. I went to this school for three years.

Later, the United States Central Intelligence Agency (CIA) hired new teachers for the Hmong people in the mountains, and I attended their school. In this CIA school I learned about maps and how to use a compass to find directions. I learned how to shoot a big gun. I learned to take a gun apart, clean it, and put it back together. I learned how to throw hand grenades.

At this time there were about three million people in Laos. These people spoke many different languages, including Hmong, Laotian, Dao, Chao, and Eako. About one million of the people were Hmong. There were five main generals for the Royal Lao Army in Laos. Four of them were Laotian and one was Hmong, General Vang Pao. Vang Pao had fought alongside the French soldiers, who had been fighting the North Vietnamese communists since around 1950.

During the 1960's and early 1970's, Vang Pao worked with soldiers from the CIA. Jerry was one of the American CIA soldiers. James was another. I don't remember their last names. They controlled the Hmong soldiers in Long Chieng, the town where I lived. The CIA soldiers would communicate with the American Army and Air Force to order weapons (guns, bombs, or mines) and food (rice or meat). Whatever we needed.

In 1961 the CIA brought guns into Laos. Men in our town learned how to be soldiers. Our teachers were Thai; the CIA brought soldiers from Thailand's army to live in the Hmong villages and teach the Hmong men to be soldiers.

The Hmong soldiers lived in the mountains surrounding Long Chieng. The CIA would fly supplies and people into the area. Helicopters would fly in, and then the people would climb down a rope ladder from the helicopter to the mountain. Small planes would drop rice in the mountains. Trucks could not go in the mountains because there were no roads, so it was necessary to use planes and helicopters.

All the Hmong men, except the very old—70 or 80 years old—were soldiers.

As I said, in 1961, when I was 14, I became a soldier. I was given a regular military rifle, which was very big compared to a 14-year-old boy. When I tried to carry it, it would drag on the ground. If I tried to carry it upright and level, it would tilt down and the barrel would dig into the ground. Sometimes the barrel got blocked with dirt and leaves. Sometimes I would stumble or fall down and not be able to keep up with the other soldiers.

So the CIA gave me and the other young boys smaller guns that folded up. I could carry the folded gun. I could march and keep up. When it was time to shoot, I would unfold the gun and shoot.

In this way young boys could be good soldiers.

The uniform was also too big for me. I would pay money to have mine cut down so it would fit. Or I would use rubber bands around the cuffs to hold up the pant legs and a big belt around the waist to keep the pants from falling down.

For the first four years I was a soldier near our town. Then in 1965, when I was 17, I went on a helicopter to Long Chieng. After that, I fought alongside other Hmong soldiers in the mountains. Then I had a regular gun, a long gun, not a folding gun. The long gun had eight shells. I also used a machine gun, a 3.5 bazooka, and a gun that was referred to by number—these were light guns that were used at the front. I also used a 60 gun, a 75 gun, an 81 gun, a 150 gun, and a 155 gun—these were heavy guns that were carried in the rear.

In the Hmong Army, the language that was spoken was Lao. The CIA handlers spoke Lao well. Some of them even spoke Hmong, too.

We were in Vang Pao's Group Number Two. The King of Thailand sent soldiers to help this Group. The Hmong soldiers fought in the front. The Thai soldiers stayed in the back, helping.

In 1970 I was injured by a land mine explosion—a little mine the size of an egg. I lost part of my right leg. I spent two months in the hospital where I was cared for by Lao doctors. Now I have a plastic leg from just below the knee.

There were many mines which had been laid down by the Communist soldiers. The mines were of different sizes, the smallest being the size of an egg, which was the kind that caused my injury. The Hmong soldiers did not have mine detector devices which could have helped protect us from the mines. A lot of Hmong soldiers and other Hmong people lost their legs because of the mines.

In 1975 the Americans left Vietnam and Laos. The Communist soldiers who were in Laos said,"We are stronger. We've got it! We've got the country!"

At this time Vang Pao left Laos and flew to Thailand. He is now living in California.

The Communist soldiers required everyone in Laos to register with them. They put Hmong people into work groups, and we had to work making roads and filling shell holes. The workers had little food—one bowl of rice in the morning and one bowl at night—and many of them became sick and died. Sometimes Hmong leaders would be killed.

Many people died or were injured in the work groups. Filling the shell holes was dangerous, because they could hide live shells. The Communist soldiers would sometimes kill workers. If a worker was sick and couldn't work, the soldiers would say, "No, you are just lazy. You must work."

Because of these terrible conditions, the Hmong people wanted to leave the work groups. The Communist soldiers said, "No, don't go. Stop. Don't go." But the Hmong people said, "No, we must go." The people ran away, and the Communist soldiers shot at them.

Former Hmong soldiers went with their families to live in the jungle. I did this with my family in 1975. We lived in the jungle and continued to fight the Communists until 1980. In December 1980 we decided to leave and travel to Thailand.

We walked to Vientiane, the capital of Laos, which borders on Thailand. At the Mekong River we made a boat by tying bamboo together. One family in one boat. We arrived in Thailand on January 5, 1981.

It was dangerous getting off the boat in Thailand. Many of the Thai soldiers wanted to shoot the Hmong people. But the Thai leaders said, "No, stop; don't shoot." Most of the Thai soldiers obeyed their leaders, but some did not.

James, who had been one of the CIA handlers at Long Chieng, later was with the Joint Voluntary Association (JVA) in the camp in Thailand. The JVA interviewed Hmong people in the camp to find out if they had been soldiers, who were qualified to go to the United States. James registered the Hmong veterans to go to the United States. If you were in the camp and wanted to go to the United States, you had an interview with him.

He would show you a picture of a gun and ask, "What kind of gun is it?" He would show you a map and ask, "Where was your unit?" "Who was your officer?" "How far is it from your village to Vientiane?"

We had to answer these questions to show that we had been soldiers. Only soldiers and their families got to go to the United States. I wanted to go to the United States because I had been a soldier in the Hmong Army. The Communist soldiers would kill me if I went back to Laos.

After we registered with JVA, we had to wait a long time before we could go to the United States. We lived in the refugee camp in Thailand for seven years. In 1987 we flew to the United States, to New York. From 1987 to 1996 we lived in Syracuse, New York. Then in 1996 we moved to St. Paul, Minnesota, where we live now.

JOYCE YAMAMOTO

Recollections of the Vietnam War Period

John Wallace

I remember the Vietnam War as a terrible time in this country.

Every night on the evening news there were horrible scenes from the battle areas and from the cities in Vietnam. There were scenes, equally horrible in their way, of angry and violent protests in this country. And there were the depressing scenes of generals and elected officials trying to put the best face on what the United States was doing in that war. I and many others suspected that much of what they said was lies and deceptions.

Now we know that we were right in our suspicions.

I participated in marches and demonstrations, including some very large ones in Central Park in New York City. In these I felt powerless, that my participation was doing nothing. I marched so that I could feel like I was at least doing something—but all the time I realized that it was pretty useless. I had the sense of being in a nightmare that would never end. Then when it did end (April 30, 1975—I looked it up), when that last helicopter pulled the last Americans from the roof of the embassy in Saigon, the emotion I had was a huge feeling of relief.

"Thank God that war is over—forever; I don't have to think about it ever again; I am never going to think about it again."

And I pretty much did not think about it. In the late 1980's and early 1990's, when I was working with the college student community service movement. It struck me that these students had the same passion for making a better society that I and students I had known had had during the Vietnam War period. But their passion for justice was "sweeter and without the anger" that we had felt.

But mainly I put the war out of my mind, not thinking about it from one year to the next.

Until—and I am grateful that there is this "until"—I began to work and become friends with Hmong immigrants at the Jane Addams School in the summer of 1996. I am not sure that I had even known about the "secret war" in Laos and the part the Hmong people played in it.

At the same time we were protesting the war in Vietnam and the United States "incursion" into Cambodia, CIA "advisors" were working with Hmong guerrilla fighters in Laos. I didn't know that until long after the war was over.

With these new relationships with Hmong friends a chapter that never would have been completed is being closed. A wound that I had even forgotten I had is healing.

"There is power when people share
ideas and work together."

Koua Her

Section 3
The Road I Walked
Se Vang*
Shao Lee
Life in America
Jennifer L. O'Donoghue
Freedom Festival

JOYCE YAMAMOTO

The Road I Walked

by Jessica Smith

Citizenship Must Be Practiced

My first experience with Jane Addams School was at a community meeting held in early spring at Neighborhood House. Congressman Bruce Vento and Senator Paul Wellstone attended the meeting to answer questions and explain to the Hmong residents about welfare reform and how it affected immigrants who were not citizens.

The room we met in was crowded and hot.

Despite this, the sense of urgency and frustration that pervaded the air was stronger than that which the physical climate could suppress. Most of us who came from the university stood around the perimeter of the room, while those to whom the meeting was really directed sat shoulder to shoulder. At this first encounter I felt like an outsider peering in at the lives of strangers. I was angered by the affects that welfare reform would have on these people, but at the same time I felt separate from the people and the situation and powerless to do anything about it

I had heard from people who had worked at Jane Addams before that the Hmong circle was intense. One of my friends told me that the Hmong residents never took breaks from learning and that he left after every night exhausted. I was a bit intimidated by these reports as I walked into the upstairs room where the Hmong circle met, and I quietly sat in a corner. Again I felt like an outsider, more nervous and taller than I had ever felt before.

I don't remember who I worked with that evening, but I do remember how relieved I was that I had a list of questions from the citizenship exam in front of me, and that the Hmong resident knew the "routine" of the language practice. We started with the colors of the flag, and didn't look up until 90 minutes had passed and we were sixty some questions down the list.

Like the others before me, I, too, left exhausted, but also with tremendous excitement. This was a challenge I had never experienced before, and I reveled in the newness of the meeting and the thought that I had made it through one night. I was ready to return.

In the few weeks that followed, I began to work with two women on a regular basis. Both women, Shao and Se, were newcomers to the group and always sat together. It just became natural that I would sit down at the same table. The three of us worked well together.

Create Space for Each Person

For the first three weeks or so, we did nothing but go over the citizenship questions. I would read a portion of a question, and Shao and Se would repeat what I had said. Slowly, the two women began to work as a team. While reading, if one woman didn't know one of the words, the other would say the word for both of them and the two women would go on in unison. Although these first few weeks were relatively identical in terms of what words we looked at, in hindsight I consider them a crucial beginning for establishing our relationship and opening up a space for us to interact beyond reading the words off of the page.

This space has been an invaluable part of my encounters at Jane Addams School. When I think about my times at Jane Addams now as opposed to what they were like a year ago, I am certain that changes have occurred as the result of an increasing amount of trust between myself and those with whom I worked.

Work with Rather than For

Throughout the summer at Jane Addams, Shao, Se and I continued to work together. Over the weeks, I began to realize certain aspects of the time that I spent there had changed. One of the first things I realized, which still remains important in my interactions at Jane Addams School, was the way the three of us sat.

When I first started, it usually worked out that I would sit across the table, facing the person I was working with. I gave little thought to this way of sitting, but soon I realized that something about the way we sat wasn't right for the setting or the intentions behind our exchanges. I had sat in this configuration many times in places like doctor's offices, interviews or meetings with supervisors. In each instance, these encounters had been with people "superior" in knowledge or position to myself, and these times had been intimidating. This wasn't the relationship that I wanted to establish with Shao and Se.

It happened by chance that one evening I sat in between instead of across from them. The difference was immediately noticeable. I felt more at ease speaking and reading, and I noticed that the words from Shao and Se came from stronger, more assured voices. Instead of being an observer or outsider to their learning, I became an active participant.

Laughter played an important role in the times I spent at the school. At first, laughter was of the nervous sort that comes with uncertainty of new things. As time passed, and my relationship with Shao and Se began to find its roots, the laughter changed and sometimes took on a form that consumed our entire time working together.

One evening, Shao and Se tried to explain to me what their occupations were. As I understood it, the two women arose very early in the morning and spent their day at the airport sweeping. Twenty minutes after I heard this I asked them again about their airport jobs. Se looked at me as if I was crazy, and Shao replied to my question with a quizzical grin. I thought that they had misunderstood me, so I asked them again:

"How long each day do you work at the airport?"

Immediately, the two women erupted into fits of laughter, while I sat there trying to figure out what I had said that was so funny. Shao's daughter, who is bilingual, happened to be there during this time. It took her about five minutes to gain composure enough just to tell me that her mom and Se worked in a factory sewing and were wondering where in the world I came up with the notion that they worked in the airport.

For the rest of the night, none of us could keep our faces straight enough to practice the citizenship test.

JOYCE YAMAMOTO

Intergenerational Connection

The role which Shao and Se's children played in the learning circle was extremely valuable for the parents, the children, and me. It was helpful to have the children around while trying to explain difficult concepts to their parents. The hours that it would take me to explain the branches of government to Shao and Se could be explained in a matter of minutes by their children. Often, I have remained silent for long periods of time because the children possess such a wonderful ability to understand and speak in two languages. It has been fascinating to watch this intergenerational aspect of the learning occur. Because the experiences and perceptions of the Hmong children are often so different from that of their parents, the opportunity for the child to explain an American concept in the Hmong language to a parent provides intergenerational and multicultural common ground.

Having the child enter into the learning meant that for the first time, the phrases that Shao and Se heard me repeat over and over again began to take on some meaning. In addition, they've taken form not through English, but rather by hearing them through the words and phrases of their own children in a language that they understand.

As Shao and Se continued to bring their children with them throughout the summer I was repeatedly reminded of how flexible learning can actually be. It can be stretched and pulled and re-shaped until everyone fits into its folds. Why is it that we rely on manuals and worksheets when parents and children can learn together so easily?

Everyone's a Teacher, Everyone's a Learner

I had been learning immense amounts from teaching Shao and Se, but one evening, Shao decided to take on the role of teacher quite spontaneously.

I was trying to explain the part of the citizenship exam that deals with the Bill of Rights. When I was done explaining the third amendment, it was very clear that Se had no idea what it was that I was trying my hardest to explain. Shao, who said she understood "a little," turned to explain in Hmong what she could to Se. I soon realized, however, that when Shao turned her head back in my direction, she was still speaking in Hmong. She did this for about ten seconds more before she realized what language she was speaking. I thought the whole situation to be very funny, and I assumed that she would try to explain what she had just said to me in English.

I was wrong.

Within seconds, Shao resumed her conversation with me in Hmong. I didn't know what to do, so I just sat there and let her finish what she had to say. When I told her that I didn't understand, she explained to me in Hmong again what she wanted me to do. Finally, after spending five minutes shrugging my shoulders and racking my brain to figure out what she was saying, Shao took the page we were working on, turned it and began to read from the next page. Then she said again that phrase that I had heard numerous times in the previous five minutes.

She was saying to me: "Turn the page and read."

We Are All Engaged in the Co-Creation of JAS

At the end of the summer, I left Minneapolis to go to visit my parents for a few weeks. Upon returning, I immediately jumped into a hectic schedule of work and school. For awhile, Jane Addams School seemed too far out of reach. I just didn't feel as if I had the time to add going there back into my schedule. After a while though, I realized I missed the feeling of being connected to the School and the women with whom I worked, so I returned.

The progress Shao and Se had made in terms of their English seemed leaps and bounds ahead of where they started, and they were becoming increasingly proactive in deciding how they wanted to work. Our connection was one that I knew I needed.

All Cultures are Honored

Soon after I returned, Se and I sat down to talk about how she got from Laos to the United States. She told the story of her husband as a soldier during the Vietnam War.

I sat there completely silent as she talked of how her village was blown up and her husband was shot to death because the Communists in Laos had been told of their presence. She had escaped with her children into the forest only to be caught a month later by the government, almost dead of starvation. Se raised her children as best she could by herself and farmed a small plot of land to feed themselves. After years had past, Se had managed to save enough money to try to escape with her children again. This time they made it almost all of the way to the border of Thailand when soldiers who were on the road robbed them. They lost everything, and again, were forced into the jungle to hide. They moved by night, and stayed alive by drinking the water that collected on the leaves. In the year 1979, after two days of hiding in the jungle, Se and her children crossed the Me Kong River into Thailand.

At the end of her story, Se removed a picture from her purse. On the back, it was inscribed to her and contained a few words of Hmong that I did not understand. The front was a picture of her husband in uniform.

She asked if I would help her to write a letter to the American government. She wanted to tell how her husband lived and died as result of being a soldier during the secret war. I agreed to help her write this, and See Moua, a bilingual college student, agreed to help translate Se's words into English.

A month and a half passed before I had the opportunity to help Se with the letter. On that evening, I walked into Neighborhood House and found Se standing by the door outside the room we usually sat in. I greeted her as I normally did, and she responded with a quiet "hi" and a subdued smile. She followed me into the room and we sat together with Shao who was already there.

It soon became apparent by the murmuring of the women who surrounded Se that something wasn't right with her. With the help of a translator, the few of us who didn't speak Hmong were told that she had pains in her chest and was having difficulty breathing. Se had said that she had had these pains before, and that she did not want to have a doctor called. One of the women had Tiger Balm that she rubbed into her chest, but after about 15 minutes, the pain had not gone away. We told her that we would call an ambulance, and she said very little except to ask for her son who was also there that evening. When the ambulance arrived, Se and her son left and I followed behind to wait with the boy until the rest of the family arrived at the hospital.

This was the last I saw of Se.

I only heard occasional, vague updates as to how she was doing. The letter that I was to help her write was never written; but her story will forever be in my mind as I think of her smile and the sense of quiet strength that she carried about her.

Build a Vibrant, Intellectual Culture Grounded in the Everyday Experiences of Jane Addams School and the Connection to Larger Issues

In the weeks that followed, Shao and I returned to our normal routine of the learning exchange. At first, without Se there, Shao seemed a little less confident in her reading and talking with me. It took awhile before I noticed that her assertiveness re-appeared.

One day while we were going over a list of possible exam sentences, Shao and I started to talk about her work. One of the questions read, "I like to go to work." Jokingly, I asked her if she agreed with this statement and was somewhat surprised when she responded with a firm "No!"

She went on to tell me that her work had recently changed management. Due to these changes, she would no longer be given the two weeks paid vacation that she'd always gotten through the company. This announcement basically meant that she wouldn't be able to take any time off, whether it was for a vacation or to go on her children's field trips. When Shao approached her supervisor, she was told that she could either quit her job or choose to keep quiet about the whole situation.

I was angry about this, so I spent some time trying to figure out any way to prove that the company was in the wrong. Three weeks later, I hadn't gotten far except to find out that there were no laws to protect the workers from decisions like the one the management had made with their vacation time. At Jane Addams School, I asked Shao again how her work was going, and she replied that everything was fine.

After a bit more prompting, she added that she had gotten her two weeks of vacation back, and would be given an additional week the following year. Then she said that she and several other workers in her department had gotten together and approached the supervisors telling them that if they didn't get the vacation, they would all leave. As a whole, their work was extremely valuable to the company, and it would have been a serious setback to train an entirely new crew.

"Shao," I said, "do you realize that what you did is an example of what it means to live in a democracy?"

The word that she had struggled with for months had finally taken shape in her own life. When Shao and I first started to work together, the words that she read off the pages of the citizenship exam were just that: words. Finally, this concept took on it's own meaning for Shao because she was involved directly in the meaning of the word. Even now, it would still be difficult for Shao to tell me what democracy means in terms of a dictionary definition, but I am certain that she knows what the word means when she reads it off a page.

People are Known by Name, by Their Talents and Contributions

When Shao, Se and I first started working together, we very seldom got beyond "How are you?"

It took months before Shao went further than this point. At first, on being asked a question that didn't relate to the exam, Shao would say, "I don't know how to talk to you." And that was it.

Gradually, she began to respond to my questions. At first she would say her customary, "I don't know how to talk to you." Then she would go on to answer my question.

Subsequently, she started to ask questions of me. When we started having questions outside of the exam questions, Shao seemed more at ease talking with me, and her English improved.

Reflections

One of the most impressive conversations that Shao and I had throughout the year centered around her ideas on the importance of education. One evening, I asked Shao what freedom meant to her, and what she tried to pass on to her children. She began by saying:

Freedom meant being able to do what her heart desired; that in Laos this was not available to women because the men were so dominating.

She said that she told her three daughters:

Value education, because if you were in Laos, you would be working in fields.

She told me, "I want my children to use me as an example. I was deprived of an education. They should feel proud that they can get one here."

Indeed, Shao had tried both in Laos and Thailand to learn to read and write, but she had been unable to because of the cost, and because she was a woman. Now that her children are older, she can afford the time to spend a few hours each week to come to Jane Addams. It's taken months, but now Shao has even begun to exercise her own freedom through her education. The education that she stresses to her children is now accessible to her.

It is hard to believe that the year at the Jane Addams School has passed so quickly. In some ways, very little of my experience there has changed. I continue to leave each time exhausted, and I continue to feel a great sense of enjoyment and energy.

In other ways, much has changed.

I've had the opportunity to develop relationships with people whom I look forward to seeing on a regular basis. I have gone from considering myself a helpless outsider to thinking of myself as part of a community. I have been humbled through hearing the stories of many of the Hmong residents and have developed through this experience a new definition of bravery, persistence and hope.

JOYCE YAMAMOTO

Se Vang*

* The name Se Vang is a pseudonym.

My name is Se Vang. I don't know the year that I was born, but the day was exactly one month after my father died. My five brothers and sisters and I helped my mother farm corn in a small city in Laos.

I was in my middle teens when the Vietnam War started. In the same year that General Vang Pao became the Hmong leader, I was married to a man named Chue Xiong. Soon after we wed, we moved to a different town. I lived in this town with my husband's relatives until the end of the Vietnam War in 1975. In the meantime, my husband became a soldier in the Hmong army and fought on the side of the United States.

After the war ended, we moved to Long Chieng to live because we were too poor to flee the country. In Long Chieng, some people reported to the government that my husband and his brother were Hmong soldiers in hiding. Soon after this, the village of Long Chieng was bombed by the Communists.

My husband and his brother were captured and shot by the soldiers of the Communist army. I thought that I could drag him to safety, but he was too weak and made me leave him behind. I fled with my two children and my husband's brother's two children into the jungles. We did not even have time to bury the bodies of my husband, his brother or any one else killed during the bombing.

For one week, I hid with my children in the jungle. There was no food or water, so we ate nothing. After a while, we caught up with my sister and some other people in hiding. My sister had a bag of rice that she shared with the children and myself. Soon after, we found a village where we could get a small amount of food. We took what we could and headed back into the jungles, but people were dying of illness and starvation. There was no chance of surviving this way in the jungle much longer, and we were not even close to Thailand.

We had no choice but to head back to the village that we had fled and turn ourselves in to the Communist troops. On our way back to the village, my niece collapsed due to starvation and died.

When we returned to the village, we turned ourselves into the chief. He enslaved us and made us pledge loyalty to him and the Communist army. The Communists were very strict with us, but they gave us food and water—more than we had seen in a long time. After one week we were moved to a larger village where many other Hmong were also enslaved. This town soon diminished in size, as there were many who escaped to Thailand or moved out of the village.

Eventually, because the town became so small, and I was only a

woman with young children, the Communist soldiers left me to do as I wished. I stayed in the village and farmed some land that people had left behind. My children were yet too young to help, so my nephew and I were the only ones who could support my family.

A long time passed, and I had saved up enough money for my family to flee to Thailand, so one night we left the village. On our way south, we were spotted by a Communist soldier and were forced to surrender all of our money as well as my jewelry in exchange for our lives and the soldier's silence.

Again we were forced to flee and hide in the jungle, this time for four days. We had to wait on the banks of the Mekong River for two days because the currents were too strong to cross. We had no food, no water and no money so we drank only water caught by leaves and petals.

In 1979, we crossed the Mekong River into Thailand and stayed in the refugee camps until 1981.

While in Thailand, I married my husband's oldest brother so that I would have a way to get to this country. I moved with my new family to the United States and had three more children.

Five years ago, I got a job in a sewing factory and have worked there ever since. My oldest children who were born in Laos have since married and live near by. My three youngest children and I live alone, and I work to support them.

Life here has been very hard. I just underwent an operation where part of my lung was removed, and getting around is not always easy. Some days, I cannot go to work. I am worried about how I will be able to continue caring for my children if I can no longer work because my husband and I are no longer married.

It is important for me to learn English not only for myself, but for my children as well.

Shao Lee

I was born in the mountains of Laos in 1968. When I was just two months old, the Communist troops raided my family's home, and we were forced to flee to a nearby village. My parents farmed in this village. While we were there, they had five more children. In total, I had four sisters and two brothers.

My family continued to farm until the Communists came to this village several years later. Again, we were forced to flee. We ran to a village near the Mekong River. We arrived there without my two younger sisters and a brother. They had been shot and killed by the Communist soldiers during the raids. My family began to farm in this area, and they continue to do so today.

When I was a teenager, my friends decided one night that they would swim across the Mekong River. I swam with them, not knowing that I would never be able to return to my home. I thought that we were just going to swim over for the night and return home the next day. When we arrived in Thailand, the country across the Mekong River, my friends told me that I would not be able to go home. I radioed my parents to let them know that I was in Ban Vinai, the refugee camp where I would spend the next six years.

Almost immediately, I got a job sewing in the camp, so I was able to make a little money. I wanted to go to school, to learn English while I was in the camp, but I didn't have enough money for that. The teachers would not allow anyone without a husband or family into their schools, so I was not able to go. In 1986, two years after arriving in Thailand, I married a man from Laos. My husband's family owned some small shops in Ban Vinai that I had been working in. I had my first two children, two girls, while still living in the refugee camp.

My older sister had fled to Thailand when I was still very young. One day, I received word that she and her husband were living in the United States. They became our sponsors, and we applied to come to the United States. In 1990, my husband, my two children and I left Thailand to meet my sister in California. We stayed with my sister for a short while before moving. My husband had a lot of family and friends living in Minnesota, so one day we boarded a Greyhound Bus and moved here. I had my third child just after arriving in St. Paul.

My life here has been very busy. When we first arrived my husband worked almost every morning and went to school every night to get his GED. Now he has his GED, and he works long hours in a factory making dental appliances. I spent many years raising my three daughters, who are now eleven, eight and six. Now I have a job sewing in a factory. I make less money now that I am working full-time than I did when I was receiving assistance and food stamps. I want to work because I don't want to live on welfare, but I can see why some people don't want to work harder to make less money. My husband makes more money than I do, so he pays for the rent and the bills; I use my salary to buy food and clothes for my daughters.

I also send money to my mother in Laos. My parents are divorced, and my dad remarried. He and his new wife have their own children now. My mom lives with my brother. Life is hard for them because they are farmers and they don't have a lot of money. So I send as much as I can to them, to help them buy the things they need. Last year I sent about $2,000 to them. My husband is not always happy that I send them this money, but I feel that I have to. They are my family, and if I can help them, then I must do it.

My children are old enough now to look after themselves for a short while, so I have the time to do something that I have always wanted to do—learn English and become an American citizen. In Laos, there wasn't much freedom for women because the culture was dominated by men. Women weren't able to go to school. Here, if I want to, I can go to school, I can learn English. To me, freedom in the United States means being able to do what your heart desires.

I work hard every day studying for the citizenship test. I come to Jane Addams School on Mondays and Wednesdays, and I go to another school on Tuesdays and Thursdays. On the weekends, I listen to tapes and practice reading the questions. I want to be a citizen very badly, but I worry that I will not pass the test. My mother is very old, and I am afraid that I will not have a chance to see her before she is gone forever. We send pictures and cassette tapes to each other, but I have not seen her face to face since I left Laos in 1984. As soon as I become a citizen, I am going to go to Laos to see her, to hold her hand.

There are some basic skills and values that I try to pass on to my children. From Laos, I try to teach them about cooking and Hmong values and customs. I also stress to them the importance of education. My children should feel fortunate to have a free education. In Laos, only people with money can afford education, and most of the mountain villages where the Hmong live are too far away from the major villages that have schools. I tell my children that if they were in Laos today, instead of going to school, they would be working in the fields. Here, they have the opportunity to be as well educated as everyone else. I want my children to learn from my lack of education just how important it really is. They should feel proud.

I also recognize that my daughters are growing up in America; they are Americans. So it is important for me to learn about American culture. When I go to Jane Addams School, I ask the American women, the college students, about their lives and their cultures. They can help me to understand the life that my daughters may have. This way I can see what life will be like for them as they grow up in this new country.

This way I can help them to be good Hmong women and good Americans too.

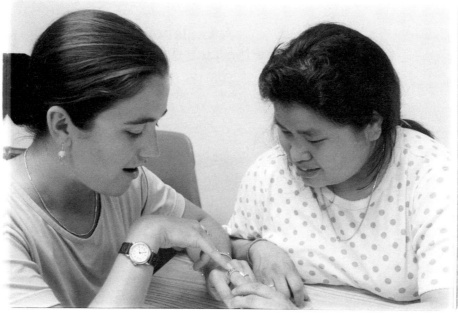

"Life in America"

A Collaborative Poem
by the Jane Addams School
Creative Writing Group

When we come to America
It's difficult
Don't know how to write in English
Don't know how to speak English
Don't know how to use things

Pay money every time
You buy something
Going to school for good education
To store or to the park
Still Hmong
Sleep late
Summer school

Drink different kinds of drinks
Coca-Cola
Sprite

St. Paul, MN
It's cold
Snow
Christmas
Listen to Hmong songs a lot

Farm in the summer
Grows rice and wild rice

Find home to live
I live on Lafond
Public housing
Housing projects

Fall
Halloween
Wear costumes
Get candy

Thailand and America
Have different houses
No job to do
Speak Hmong a lot

It's rich in America
Wearing new shoes

Driving a car
School is boring. It is not fun
I do homework
Math is boring
Gym is fun
Playing outside is fun

Holidays
Hmong New Year
Turkey Thanksgiving
Hanukkah
Happy Halloween

Burger King
Perkins
A lot of food
Hamburger
Pizza
French-fries
Chicken nuggets

Some people are rich and
Some people are not
Some people speak different languages than
Other people
Different faces
Different names
Dress different
Cut hair
Some people have different skin than us
Some people wear different shoes
Different designs on clothes

Thailand have houses
And so does America
Big family lives in America

Hmong are nice and mean
Tan skin

See the sky Moon
And a lot of stars you can see

Jennifer
L. O'Donoghue

The biggest influence in my life has been my mom.

My parents got divorced when I was too young to even remember it, and I grew up without really having my dad around. In some ways it was really hard to grow up with just my mom, but in a lot of other ways I feel like I was really blessed because my mom is such an incredible person. She has taught me so much through her own experiences—the life that she has lived and what she has gone through.

She struggled with being a single mother and raising three really little kids. I was not quite two and my brothers were about four and five when my parents got divorced, so she went through a lot taking care of us and raising us pretty much on her own. We moved to Minneapolis where we didn't really know anyone; we didn't have any family or anything to help.

I think that was really hard for her. She went through times where other people told her how she should raise her children. She tells this story of being called into my nursery school by the director and having the director sit her down and say, "Now mom...," that's what she called her, "These are the things that you need to do. Do this, not that, mom." And the neighbors were always giving her trouble because I liked to run around without any shoes on.

I don't think we were easy kids for my mom to raise!

Growing up, we didn't have many rules in our house, but we did have a few. My brother was kind of an angry child sometimes, and he would scream and swear, and I don't think my mom liked that, but she never said to us, "Oh you can't swear, you can't do that." But there were some things we weren't allowed to say in our house—hateful, derogatory words. For example, when we were younger, we used to say "fag" a lot because we didn't know any better. She would sit down with us and explain how words like that can cause people pain. She taught us to think about what words really mean and the pain they can cause.

So much of what I've experienced in my life I can connect back to my mom. She has gone through many changes in her life as far as what it means to be a woman, and has helped me to be strong and believe in myself. I think that my deep connection to community and struggling against injustice and oppression has come from her. She taught me through example the importance of making sure that we create the societies that we want to live in and that we want our children to live in.

She has also been so supportive of the decisions I've made in life. When I wanted to go away to college, I really wanted to leave Minnesota. She took me on a "seventeen-colleges-in-ten-days" tour of the East Coast. And when I was scared, she always said, "It's gonna be ok. You can do it. Believe in yourself." So when I went away for college she was behind me all the way. The same thing was true when I went to study in Australia. She was so excited, she even came to visit me.

When I was in Australia I told her that I was going to travel in Southeast Asia. She encouraged me to do that; she had lived there for two years when she was younger, working with the Peace Corps. After I finished college, I thought, "What am I going to do now? Maybe I'll go back to Thailand." And she was 100% behind me doing it. Other people asked me, "Why do you want to do this? Why do you want to go to all these other places? What is there that we don't have here?" But my mom just said, "Go! Go! Go! Follow your dream!" Of course she also likes it because she gets to come visit me wherever I am – see penguins in Australia, ride all over Thailand on the back of a motorcycle.

When I was in high school I had what I would call a "moment of awakening."

My senior year, we filled out these student council surveys in our homerooms that asked what we thought would improve the school and how student council could work better. I was taking them up to the student council office afterwards, and I started looking through them, reading them. I'd known the people in my homeroom for four years, and some of them I was pretty close with. So it really shocked me when I read what they'd written to the question "How can we improve the work of the student council?"

I looked at the first one and it said, "Get rid of the nigger president." I was stunned—"What?!"—and I tried to think of who in my homeroom would write that. I turned to the next one, and it said the same thing. Again and again. Half of the sheets, half of the people in my homeroom were saying this. It really shocked me, and I didn't know what to do. I was holding all these papers, and I just thought, "There's no way that I can go and give these papers to this person, and have him read that this is what people think about him." So I threw them all away in this big garbage can.

In a lot of ways that shocked me out of some stupid naivete that I had had. I think I had believed that there wasn't a lot of racism and stuff going on in our school. But that was a really important moment for me in terms of questioning the status quo and not accepting that just because things seem peaceful, they are. Peace or quiet can just be a cover for what's really going on, and we need to be aware of what is happening underneath that.

When I went away to Wesleyan for college, people talked about these issues more, and I loved it. This pushed me even more in the direction of not just accepting things the way they are. I learned about the importance of really thinking through and coming to terms with what I believe and then taking a stand in support of those beliefs, which isn't always easy.

The biggest decision, to date, in my life, was deciding to go work in a refugee camp in Thailand after college.

When I first thought I would go to Thailand, it was to do a very different kind of job—working in a university. But then Lucy and Jess, two of my college roommates who had been travelling in Southeast Asia, called and said, "You have to come and work in this refugee camp. You can volunteer for now. They'll be hiring in a few months, and hopefully you'll be able to get a job then." It was a hard decision—to go half-way around the world with no job or anything. But I went. I think I was there for about a week or so before I started volunteering. Then after a few months I started working—paid work.

I remember my first few days in Thailand so well. It was a terrifying experience! First, there was the fact of being in a country where I couldn't speak the language, couldn't even say hello to anyone. Lucy and Jess went to work early in the morning and didn't get home until around 6:30 at night, and I stayed at home thinking, "What am I going to do?" The first three days that I was there I was so scared, that I just stayed in the house. We didn't have any food because we didn't have a refrigerator or anything, so I didn't eat. I just stayed there, inside, afraid to go out the door. But finally I realized that I couldn't do that, so I went out to the market. I remember the first thing I bought was corn on the cob. I pointed at it and handed the woman some money, and she had this huge smile on her face, so I'm sure I gave her about ten times what it cost.

When I talk with the Hmong women at Jane Addams School now, they have similar stories of their first days or weeks in the United States. And they laugh when I tell them my story, but I think they laugh because they really understand it, they relate to it. It's so scary trying to navigate your way when you're in a place where you don't even know how to communicate. You can just feel so lost, so adrift.

For the first few months in the camp I was a volunteer, working in the Child Development Center (CDC). The way the camp was set up, they had different programs for different ages, and the CDC was for the kids who were five and under. At first I was just working in the office. Then the CDC started a class for Hmong elders, because the adult classes in the official program only went up to age 55. The first day I went to teach, they handed me this big wooden clock with movable hands and said, "Ok, go in and teach them about time." Oh, I was scared—"Aaah!! What???" I didn't know what to do. I'd been a teaching assistant for psychology classes in college, but that was of no help in this situation. I'd never before stood up in front of a group of people where we had no common language whatsoever. But there I was, supposed to teach them about time. It was scary, but it didn't go as badly as it could have been.

Within about two days, I was in love with teaching.

Another big turning point for me, a huge choice, was deciding to stay in Thailand.

I had applied to graduate school programs in clinical psychology before I left, and so the plan was that I would stay in Thailand for eight or nine months and then come back and go to graduate school. But that's not what happened. New Year's in Thailand, which is in April, was an incredible time period for Lucy, Jessica, and me. We'd been there long enough that we could speak Thai pretty well, and we went on vacation to Ko Chang, an island in eastern Thailand near the Cambodian border. It was my favorite place to go. We took the bus down, and then we had to spend the night in town before we could take the boat out to the island. It was pretty much the first time that we were able to speak Thai while we were travelling, and we really talked with people. When we got to the town, there was this huge party for the New Year —which involved everyone throwing a lot of water on each other—so we went out and met all these people and just hung out and talked with them.

A few days later I was lying in a hammock on the island, and I remember thinking, "I'm having so much fun. It's too bad that I have to go back." And then all of the sudden I said to Lucy and Jessica, "Why do I have to go back to the United States? I'm so happy here."

In many ways I felt like going to the camp and working with the Hmong people there was like finding home. I say that to some people and it seems kind of weird, kind of contrived or something. But it was amazing to me how comfortable I was. There was a strong sense of community and the importance of relationships. There were all these people who even in the midst of so much hardship, suffering, and struggle had so much to give. And the feeling of being welcomed into all of that was so different from anything else I'd ever experienced.

Added to that was this experience at New Year's of finally feeling like we were connecting with Thailand too, the country that we were living in. I wasn't ready to give up on that connection. I felt like I had to push it. If I just left after six or eight months, then it would have been a great experience, but I never would have been able to go deeper. I wouldn't have been able to learn more. I wanted to feel like I was a part of the place where I was living, instead of just a visitor. So making the decision to stay was really important for me—and for my future.

After the camp closed the following year, we went to Vietnam and Laos to visit some of our friends from the camp who had repatriated and some of the relatives our students had left behind when they fled to Thailand. That was really powerful—being in Laos and seeing the bomb craters brought to life in a very deep way the stories our students had told us.

My last week in Thailand was really important for me.

I went back to Ko Chang, the same island, and stayed by myself. It was a very introspective time. I was preparing myself to come back to the United States, so I didn't really spend much time talking or getting to know other people. I spent a lot of time writing in my journal – sitting in my hammock in front of my little hut on the beach – or just floating in the water. That was one of my favorite things to do, just float in the Gulf of Thailand.

I was getting myself ready to come back.

I was kind of freaked out about coming back to the US. On the plane from Taiwan to California, they showed CNN newsclips from the US, and it was so bizarre. I was watching it, and I just started crying. I was so upset and was sobbing and sobbing. The airline had messed up my vegetarian food, so I didn't have anything to eat for this 12-hour plane ride, and the woman next to me thought I was upset about the food. She kept offering me her bread, trying to make me feel better.

> "Oh, it's going to be ok. Here, eat this."
> "It's not about the food."
> "Well what is it about?"

But I couldn't even begin to explain to her how I felt like America was crashing into me. Like it was attacking me or hitting me with a sledge-hammer or something. For a year and a half, I hadn't really experienced anything of American culture or media. I hadn't been a part of news, politics, the sensationalism of it all. I didn't even know about the whole OJ Simpson thing! I remember that one of the CNN stories they showed was about the climbing murder rate in some US city. There were graphic images of the violence – bodies lying on the sidewalks and police lights. And I just thought, "I'm not ready for this. I can't do it. I just can't." It was really scary.

My second day back in the US, my brother took me to the supermarket. He said, "Buy whatever you want. You can eat whatever you want." But I just looked around this huge store and these aisles and aisles of food towering over me, and I started crying. It was just too much.

These decisions reflect a constant struggle in my life.

I've always had to fight between feeling like I'm settled, just going along with what I'm doing, and feeling like I need to push myself, to challenge myself to find something more. To reach beyond being settled. That was why I went to Thailand in the first place. Then after I came back and had worked for a little over two years, I struggled with these feelings again. Finally I decided I had to go to something new. I just realized that I had to push myself to think more about what I was doing, to find out more about my path, my calling. That's why I started graduate school.

Connecting to Jane Addams School and the work at the Center for Democracy and Citizenship has helped me to pursue my path, and also to see the ways in which I had been running away from it. When I first came back I thought, "I'm NOT going to be a teacher!" because I really didn't want to be involved in education. But now, seeing how important education is to me, I can't imagine not being involved in it. I couldn't see that before because of the ways that I viewed education and teaching – the teacher in the front, having all the knowledge. Learning to see education in different ways from how it's traditionally presented has been really important for me.

Also, Jane Addams School has helped me to see and feel the importance of connecting the learning of the "classroom" to the outside world—taking the strength of the community that you build within the time and space of the school and stretching it and putting it to use in other venues. You need to make it a part of your life and the life of the community. It's about having a broader effect than just saying "Ok, these are the learning objectives, and now that you've reached them the class is over and you're done."

Another big struggle for me has been learning how to be myself.

On a personal level, this has probably been my biggest challenge – being able to feel comfortable enough to be myself and to allow who I really am to be seen by other people. In high school I felt like I couldn't be who I really wanted to be. I didn't let many people know the real me. Maybe high school is just generally like that. There's such a tension between wanting to learn and wanting to be liked; wanting to be myself and wanting to fit in. For me, it has to do with the struggle to believe in my own voice and to feel like I deserve to have that voice heard in public.

My time spent in Thailand, away from all the pressures of what I would call "mainstream American society" was critical in helping me with this struggle. Being away from that was really good in terms of my developing and trusting more in my own voice, trusting that I could be the person that I wanted to be and not fit into some other preconceived notion of who I should be.

Teaching actually helped me with this a lot too. It was a very liberating thing for me in terms of believing in my voice. I remember when my mom came to visit me in Thailand, she came to one of my classes, and she was amazed. Afterwards she said, "I can't believe that this is the same you. My daughter, my little baby who is so shy and so quiet is getting up there in front of so many people." Teaching in some ways was like getting on stage and performing. It really helped me to unleash my silent voice—to be able to get up and stand in front of people and talk.

Plus, having the challenge of being in a new place, I could push myself to become me. There weren't other people's preconceived notions about me holding me back. I could reinvent myself. It's not a total reinvention though. It's almost like letting out the really important stuff that other people couldn't see before.

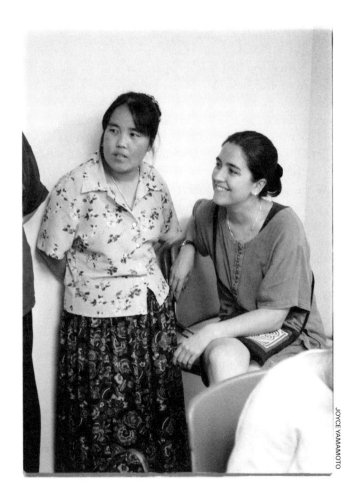

JOYCE YAMAMOTO

I never really thought about what my own culture was until I left the US, until I was living in another culture.

I guess I never really thought, "Am I this, am I that?" If people asked me, I would say I'm Irish just because my last name is Irish, but really Irish isn't even the largest percentage of what I am, and I don't know anything about what it means to be Irish or what Irish culture is. When I went to Thailand, for the first time I experienced being different from the majority culture, being thought of as an outsider, and being lumped into a category. And the really interesting thing was that when I got there, people didn't believe that I was American because I don't have blonde hair and blue eyes. I would tell people I was from the US, and they'd say, "No, no, where were you born or where are your parents from originally? You're not really an American, your hair's not blonde, your eyes aren't blue." It was weird.

Then there were other things like people saying that they couldn't tell my friend Lucy and me apart. Here's me, a five-foot-five, black-haired, brown-eyed, olive-skinned woman and this like six foot tall, strawberry-blonde, pale as can be, blue-eyed woman, and they were saying they couldn't tell us apart?! I always thought that was really odd, even unbelievable. Many times people told us that our skin was ugly. Thai people used to come up to me and touch my skin, touch my arm and say, "Ugh, it's so white. It's so ugly."

This kind of thing was so foreign to me. In a lot of ways it was really painful, but I don't think I could ever have had a better experience in terms of understanding what it's like not to be a part of the majority culture. It also helped me to understand that I don't want to accept that there really is a majority culture in the US. I don't want to accept a culture that alienates people who can't or don't want to fit in. I won't accept that the "majority culture" can or should be "the" culture of America. Also, being a person who people would identify as part of that majority culture, I feel like I have a really important role in cracking that open, in "outing it" so to speak. I have to say, "This isn't ok. This isn't the way it should be." I have that responsibility.

Last year I had to write a paper about my family for school, and for the first time I saw that I have a very specific culture too. I learned so much about my family background and can see now how that shapes my culture and who I am. It's mostly about education and strong women. So many women in my family, through the generations, have had to raise families and take care of children and educate themselves without necessarily having a male partner around. I learned that I'm in the fourth generation of women in my family to go to college. I told someone that and they said, "Well you must feel really special then."

He said it very sarcastically, like "Oh, aren't you privileged?" But I thought, "No, it's not about privilege." It's about my great-grandmother getting up every morning to do her farm chores before getting herself to college. It's about women who struggled in what was basically an all-male space. It's about hard work and recognizing the importance of education, especially for us as women, if we want to change our world.

To me, that's my family's culture—educating yourself, but also being involved in education and the creation of the community. It has been really important for me to learn this. A friend once told me that until you know your own story, you can't really listen to anyone else's. Learning about my own history has allowed me to really hear other people.

As I get older, I think a lot about what I would want to teach my children, what culture to pass down to them. It's hard for me to put a finger on it, to name what it is. One thing that comes to mind is teaching them to be who they are, who they want to be. It's not really so much teaching as it is about my role as a parent in creating ways for them to be who they are. I would hope to teach them the importance of loving and respecting people as people. Trying to see beyond the different ways that we're taught to divide ourselves from other people to just loving and understanding people as people.

One thing that I really want for my kids is for them to grow up in a supportive and extended community. I was saying to someone awhile back that I would love for my kids to be really connected to my friends in the Hmong community, to have all these "aunts" and "uncles" and "cousins." When I see how close and supportive many Hmong families are, I want my kids to have something like that. And I would love for them to be bilingual. But it's not just about them knowing Hmong culture or language, it's about knowing that there are so many different ways to be in this country.

The Freedom Festival will always be the biggest single story from JAS for me.

I learned so much through that experience. The most important lesson I learned in organizing that day was that the critical thing is to create the space. You create the space, and then people come and do with it what they want. D'Ann and I kind of knew the general things that would happen that day, but so much happened that we could never have planned. So organizing that day was really just about saying, "Ok, there's going to be this space, and come and turn it into what you want it to be." And they did. The Hmong women brought food and were giving it away—"Free Hmong Food!" Lia filled the park with her beautiful and heartbreaking songs. The kids blew everyone away with their performance and reading their letters.

Definitely one of the most moving moments of that day was when we had the ceremony to honor new citizens, and John was talking about Lee Her. He was saying how privileged he was to be able to work with Lee and what Lee had taught him about what it means to be a citizen and an American. Lee was standing next to me, and when I looked over at him, he was crying. His face was stoic and strong, but he had these tears just slowly running down his face. I will never forget the power of that moment.

Another big part of JAS for me has been the building of my relationship with Shao. Sometimes the time that we have spent together has been silly time—laughing and sharing funny stories. At other times it's serious and sad. It's also hard work on the citizenship test or learning Hmong. It's Shao spending hours with me teaching me how to sew paj ntaub. It's the two of us going to shop for purses at "Old Navy." It's so multilayered.

After I graduate, I'm moving to California. I'm excited, but when I think of leaving JAS and the important relationships I've become a part of there, it hurts. Even if you have a really hard day, being in this community can energize you. I'll walk into JAS, and Na Cha Lee and See Cha Lee will run up yelllng, "Paj Kub! Paj Kub!" , and I'll know I'm really at JAS. And it's not just the fact that people there know you, it's that you are accountable to them and the work of the School. If you're not there, the next night people will come and ask you "Where were you?" It's all these things, that words can't even explain, that just become a part of you.

I've learned so much about freedom over the past six years.

I think it was probably something that I didn't think about that much before I went to Thailand. I'm sure it was something I thought about in terms of the lessons my mom taught me or in terms of realizing that there are many people in the United States and the world who aren't as free as other people. But my thinking was kind of superficial.

But my time in Thailand was just incredible in terms of learning lessons about life and about the meanings of freedom. I saw what it means in such a visceral, everyday way, getting on a bus every morning and riding into an area that was surrounded by armed guards and barbed-wire fences. I really had to think about what it meant to work with people who lived in that situation; what it meant to work with kids who had been born into it. Their entire lives had been behind that barbed-wire. To them, freedom meant coming to America—the promised-land. Some of the older people were scared, but to the younger people, kids who'd never been outside the barbed-wire, it really was going to be the place where they would have a life, have freedom.

I experienced that kind of "in your face" freedom and denial of freedom for the first time over there. That really prodded me to think about freedom in my own life and what that freedom means. And I see now that there is freedom *from*—from those barbed-wire fences and from the oppression and the abuse of the Thai soldiers. But there's also a very important freedom *to*—and this is something that all Americans have to see, that just because we have freedom from here, we don't necessarily have freedom to.

The story that best expresses this for me is from one of my students in Thailand who lives in Minnesota now. When his family first moved to St. Paul from Wisconsin, I went to visit them. He sat down next to me and said, "Why didn't you tell me? Why didn't you tell me that this is what it was going to be like? If I'd known, I never would have come here." And it broke my heart because when we were in Thailand, I would talk to them about America, and they looked to it as a place where they really were going to be free. But in so many ways they're not. Now it's a constant struggle of freedom to. They have freedom from now, but do they have freedom to? Do they have freedom to be themselves, to practice their cultural traditions, to participate in the creation of America? Can they become a part of this society without giving up a part of who they are? Can any of us?

I've started thinking more about these questions in terms of myself and in terms of all of us in the United States. How much freedom have I had to be who I want to be? It's really important to me to be able to be myself, to not have to give up what I think is important, to maintain my integrity, and to create the world that I want instead of having to live in the world as it is created by others. This is important for all of us.

I truly believe that the freedom of any one person is inextricably bound with the freedom of all others. Life can never be about getting freedom for yourself; it has to be about creating freedom for everyone. It has to be about opening the doors for everyone, and not just opening the doors to let people out, but opening the doors into something too. We need to continuously build ways that people can have that freedom to—to create the world, to create knowledge, to create more freedom.

West Side
Freedom Festival

Saturday, July 18
12:00 to 4:00

at Parque del Castillo
(rain site - Neighborhood House)

Featuring:

- "Elder's Wisdom, Children's Song": the youth and elders of the West Side with Larry Long and Community Celebration of Place

- Singing and Dancing!

- Handicrafts, Clothes, Food, and More!

- Appearances by Mike Freeman, Skip Humphrey, Ted Mondale, Sandy Pappas, Bruce Vento, and others

Sponsored by The Jane Addams School for Democracy and Neighborhood House

---

Gran Festival
de Libertad!

Sabado, 18 de Julio
12:00 to 4:00

en el Parque del Castillo
(en caso de llover - Neighborhood House)

Forma:

- Tendremos la actuacion de Larry Long acompanando a ninos y adultos con sus lindas canciones

- Tendremos alegres bailes y cantos

- Venderemos los trabajos manuales hechos por la comunidad

- Habra venta de ropa, comida y muchos antojitos mas

- Disfrutaremos de la compania de personas actuales en partidos politicos: Mike Freeman, Skip Humphrey, Ted Mondale, Sandy Pappas, Bruce Vento, and others

Organizado por Jane Addams School for Democracy and Neighborhood House

---

Kev Koom Ywj Pheej
"West Side"

Hnub Vaaxaum, 7 hli ntuj vaa thib 18
Lub sij hawm 12:00 txog 4:00

Tom lub tshaav ua si (phaj) hu Castillo
(has tav lug nag puab yuav ua tom lub tsev "Neighborhood House")

Yuav Muaj:

- "Cov hluas hab cov laug ntawm lub zog "West Side" (saab hnub poob) nrus "Larry Long" hab "Community Celebration of Place" hu nkauj

- Hu nkauj hab yeeb yaam!

- Khoom muas, kaab dluas, mov, hab lwm yaam!

- Num tshwv tuaj has lug le "Mike Freeman, Skip Humphrey, Ted Mondale, Sandy Pappas, Bruce Vento" hab lwm tug

Nrus qhuas hub tsiv qhuas yog hab koom luaus "The Jane Addams School for Democracy" hab lub koom luaus "Neighborhood House"

West Side Residents Celebrate at Freedom Festival

On July 18th, 1999 the Jane Addams School, together with Neighborhood House, sponsored the first annual "West Side Freedom Festival" in Parque Castillo on the West Side of St. Paul. This public celebration of freedom was a crucial way to honor the struggles of Hmong and Latino immigrants (adults and children), make visible the importance of freedom for all of us, and provide a space for children to see their parents' struggles valued. Moreover, a public celebration made our common fight for freedom come alive in a way that words alone could not.

The festival highlighted the talents and contributions of immigrants in America. At the heart of the festival was a community performance piece entitled "Elder's Wisdom, Children's Song." To create this piece, Hmong and Latino children of the West Side neighborhood worked with Larry Long, Folkways recording artist and "troubadour" from Community Celebration of Place, Inc. Larry helped the children transform their parents' struggles for freedom into spoken word, song, and dance. Other cultural events included a performance of the qeej, a traditional Hmong instrument, a piece incorporating traditional and modern elements of Latino dance, as well as songs and poetry.

Also central to the day was a ceremony publicly honoring 10 Jane Addams School members who had recently become citizens. In this way we recognized and celebrated their hard work and the contributions they have made to the School and the community. Local politicians, including Gubernatorial candidates Mike Freeman and Hubert "Skip" Humphrey, Congressman Bruce Vento and others also joined the celebration to speak about freedom and the important role of immigrants in creating and sustaining our democracy.

The success of the Freedom Festival grew out of the strength of the West Side community and the work of the Jane Addams School over the past years. The Festival reflected our philosophy that all people have talents to contribute and can be creators in our public world if presented the opportunity. The children demonstrated this as they voluntarily dedicated several hours a day in the weeks prior to the Festival for preparation and rehearsal. Larry Long, the community "troubadour" who worked with the children, was amazed by their dedication. After years of working mostly within school systems where children's participation is "mandatory," he found it refreshing to work in the Jane Addams School atmosphere.

The enthusiasm of the children was mirrored by that of their parents and others in the West Side community, who took charge of creating the character of the Festival as a whole. In addition to performances, community members set up booths displaying traditional clothing and handicrafts and offering Hmong and Latino foods, the children of the community operated a face painting booth, and the Jane Addams School booth offered participants a chance to test their knowledge of Citizenship Exam questions. The School and the residents worked to craft a Festival that reflected and enhanced the identity of the community, one which immigrants have had a critical role in creating for over one hundred years.

> "I wanted to educate people about the Hmong and Hmong culture. I wanted to show that even though we are here without a country, we have talents and can contribute."

> - Lia Yang, traditional Hmong singer

Moments from the day vividly convey the spirit of the Jane Addams School and the Festival—Hmong and Latino children, arms around each other, singing "This Land is Your Land," complete with new verses they had written; tears rolling down the cheeks of Lee Her, a veteran and new citizen, as John Wallace, his learning partner of two years, talked of Lee's contribution to the United States; the pride filling Chue Long Thao's voice as he talked of his son's qeej performance.

The pride and excitement of the community, especially of the children, as they took on a central and powerful voice in creating a festival that was truly theirs will never be forgotten. The Festival that they created conveyed to the broader community, as well as to members of the Jane Addams School itself, the deeper meaning of a "School for Democracy."

> "My favorite part was singing the song 'All the Way to Paradise' because it told our story. It told of how we came from Laos. I was kind of nervous to sing, but I was very proud."

> - Choua Xiong, Age 12

This Land is Your Land
By Arlo Guthrie
(With Verses Written by Children of the West Side)

I want freedom
For my mother
For my father
For my brother
For my sister
For one another
This land was made for you and me

Kuv xav muaj kev ywj pheej
Rau kuv niam
Rau kuv txiv
Rau kuv tus nus
Rau kuv tus muam
Rau sawv daws
This land was made for you and me

Yo quiero libertad
Para mi madre
Para mi padre
Para mi hermano
Para mi hermana
Para uno o otro
This land was made for you and me

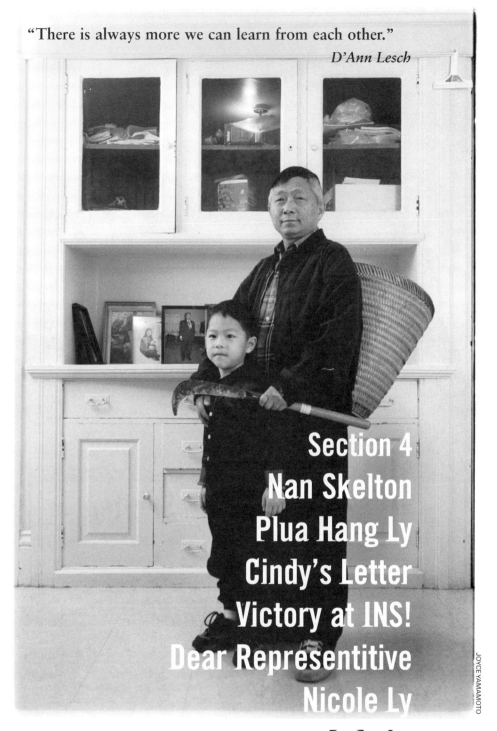

"There is always more we can learn from each other."
D'Ann Lesch

Section 4
Nan Skelton
Plua Hang Ly
Cindy's Letter
Victory at INS!
Dear Representitive
Nicole Ly
Judy Ly
D'Ann Urbaniak Lesch

Nan Skelton

When I was about ten years old, in fifth grade, I had one of those "defining moments" of life. My mother was Catholic and my father was Protestant—"non-Catholic" was what it was referred to then. That was a big deal at that time, in my generation. That was called a "mixed marriage," and it was not exactly frowned on, but close. When a Catholic and a non-Catholic married, one of the things they had to do was agree to raise their children Catholic, so I went to Catholic grade school and high school.

My father had been raised in a very strict Presbyterian religion, full of hellfire and brimstone.

"You're all going to go to hell if you dance or play cards."

He pretty much thought that was silly, so as soon as he left home that was the end of it. After that he never participated in any organized religion. As he was growing up, however, he had had to memorize the Bible, so he knew all these stories and psalms from the Bible. He could quote the Bible from one end to the other. He could also quote Shakespeare. He would mix them together, so we'd get a little Shakespeare and we'd get a little Paul, kind of stuck together. It was great. If he had a particular lesson he wanted us to learn, there would be a little "To be or not to be…" and then out would come "No greater love hath man…" We'd get these at the dinner table; we'd get them all the time.

He really loved the psalm "The Lord is My Shepherd." He would recite it to us all the time.

So, I come to fifth grade, and one day Sister Cordelia, our teacher, gave us the assignment to memorize the psalm "The Lord is My Shepherd." I thought, "Oh, Wow! This is great. I already know this, and my dad can help me with it. This is really gonna be great!" I loved the psalm; I had all sorts of memories attached to it because of my father. So I raised my hand, and I said, "Can I learn 'The Lord is My Shepherd' the way my father says it?" (He recited the psalm from the King James Version of the Bible, not the Catholic version of the Bible.)

And she went into this tirade about how wrong that was. How terrible it would be for me to ever utter the words of that psalm in anything but the Catholic version. How I would be committing a great sin. How it was really too bad that my father was a non-Catholic. She went on and on and on.

I was just ten years old, and everything in me knew that my father was a really good person. I thought his values were right, and that he had great integrity. I knew that what she was saying was wrong. This made me realize that authority is not always right. People can say things and they can prescribe things, but they're not always right.

I would do what she said, I would do it the Catholic way for the assignment, but I sure as hell wasn't going to say it that way outside of school!

This experience is one of those things that I've never forgotten. I think it instilled in me a questioning of what people say has got to be the way. I know that I need to make my own judgment. Is it "is" or is it "ain't"? It's also why I've never been good at dealing with people who want to impose their ideas, who want to convert people to their way of thinking. I'll listen, I'll take it in, but I won't swallow it whole. Conversion teaching or conversion tactics never sit very well with me.

This experience, at age ten, has affected how I choose to live my own life—what I choose to question and not—and how I want to work with students and others. I don't want to say, "There's only one way to think about this, and it's the way I think about it."

□

One of the biggest challenges I've struggled with throughout my life is not letting other people's limited expectations hold me back. If people say, "You can only do this," sometimes I will listen to them, and it stops me. I have to remember not to let that stop me.

When I was a kid, my mother used to always say, "Don't be too much—Don't be too loud. Don't read too much. Don't have too many friends. Don't stay out too late. Don't go to bed too late. Don't work too much. Don't sleep too much." The message was to be middle of the road, not be noticed. In one sense that was like putting a red flag in front of a bull. It challenged me to rebel—which was good. In another way, I had to live with the fact that somebody else's expectation was to limit myself. I've had to navigate through this.

This has been important because many of the roles that I've played in life had not been played before by women. There weren't a lot of women around doing what I was doing, and the preparation that I had been given as a woman was not the right preparation for entering into those roles. For instance, when I was Assistant Commissioner for Education, there had not been a woman in that position before. I needed to figure out how to learn the rules about how you're supposed to work in that environment.

One thing that I did a lot in those days was meet with a whole group of women from different departments. They were Assistant Commissioners and Commissioners and women legislators—both executive and legislative branch—who were in positions where they had to perform and not look silly. So we would meet for breakfast every week to coach each other. We would bring our "How do I deal with this situation?" questions. Eight or nine of us who had dealt with that situation would give suggestions or ideas. And it was amazing how we kept confidence. No one ever took what they heard there and spread it around.

□

When I think about what has gone into making me me, it has to do with memories and histories that have become part of my belief system. Some of that has come from my family and some has come from other people that I've met along the way.

My family came from Canada, and before that France and Scotland. On my mother's side, a great-grandmother was a Huron Indian. Both my parents came from rural Minnesota, so even though I never grew up on a farm or in a rural community, the traditions of rural farm life are in me through hearing their stories. My mother was one of ten children. They lived on an 18-acre farm and had about one cow—and they spoke French. The extended family—cousins and uncles and aunts—lived all around them. They were related to everybody that they knew. So that's part of what American culture is to me—rural community and extended family.

Education has been a very big part of my family too. My mother was a teacher, my sister was a teacher, and so education is also part of what American culture is for me. It's a part of my own identity—even though I fought against that. I swore I'd never be a teacher, but here I am.

The whole Catholic tradition forms another part of me, although I moved out of that organized religion piece at some point in my life. When I grew up in St. Paul, every neighborhood was organized in a Catholic parish. People went to school together, went to church together, played together. So neighborhood, what that means and how you build it, was very much part of my identity. It is tied up with Catholicism, but only because that's what it was called. For me the Catholic part was just the name that went with the meaning of being in the community.

PETER LEACH

Added to these are other influences like the anti-war movement and the civil rights movement. That whole decade had an incredible impact on shaping what I wanted to do with my life, what I thought was important. I learned a lot about what was really going on in the larger world, outside the neighborhood. And I realized that I could, and should, and must do what I could to affect that.

Then along the way came people like my friend Joyce Yamamoto— who I've known for over thirty years. She's a huge piece that gets folded into who I am. You could take any slice of me and find her there someplace. She, and many others, get mixed into who I am, and I wouldn't go against them—who they are, what they stand for, what they value, what they hold as important—because now they're part of me. Part of my integrity is to be accountable to what they've taught me, what they've given me.

All of those roots are part of me, which makes me stronger. I can't get blown off track because I've got all this rooting.

□

When my kids were little, I thought, "If they can come through this thing called growing up with a very strong sense of self-confidence then that's enough. That's it." Now I have other things I hope for them, but that was the sine qua non—that they are confident, that they are who they are, that they can do what they set their minds to do, and that they can handle what comes along. I wanted everything I did to somehow help that along, nurture that sense of confidence.

I always thought to myself, "I'd really like it if they had some of the values that I have." But I didn't want to preach at them. I was afraid if I preached at them, they'd run away from it. So it was always kind of a conundrum—how will they get it if I don't preach it? Will they get it if I just live it? And I chose to do just that. I rarely hauled them off to things. And now it's interesting to see some of the choices they make that have a lot of similarities to some of the things that I care about.

I've really wanted them to have a sense of seeing what matters and not getting caught up in the "junk." There's a lot of junk around, and if you focus on the junk, it can pull you down. You have to get beyond that. And I think they do. It's been important to me that they really follow their passion. And it doesn't have to be what I want it to be— I don't even know what I would want it to be—just as long as they have that passion and go for it. For example, John didn't have any money, so he went to Guatemala for six months. Most people thought that was pretty silly; they thought, he's a grown man, he should go to work. I thought it was more important that he do what he wanted.

☐

The period when I joined the Sisters of St. Joseph had a big impact on me. I entered the religious community to see if it was something that I wanted to do. I started when I was in my college years, and stayed for about five years. I reached a stage where I said this was good and now I need to move on.

The time there gave me the space to really understand the importance of reflection and to reflect on who I am in the world and who I want to be. I started thinking, "How am I going to do this? I need a bigger world." I couldn't be cooped up because it was what the world was calling me to do. It was not just about God, it was really about the world—not the bad materialistic world, but all that the world is and can be—and that was really important.

The next stage was to realize I could do a whole lot more than I thought I could do. I'd found my vocation. But it's not an "it." It's not something static. We're always being called to something. We can choose to respond or not respond, and in the process of that response you learn a lot about yourself and your identity, America, the world. That's an ongoing process.

☐

In the beginning, when Jane Addams School was just germinating in my consciousness, I wanted to see if a group of us could figure out a way to make learning come alive for students. I was hoping for a place where they could be engaged in real work in a community. It was frustrating for me to listen to students over and over again say things like: "Well, when I get out I will…" or "When I get into the real world I will…"

What was even more frustrating was that there was such a long period where students hadn't been connected to the real world that they were beginning to be afraid of ever being connected to it. They had no practice. It was all just kind of a mystery, very far away, very distant, and it had become mythical—either negative mythical or out of their reach mythical. I wanted to begin to bridge that so that students would be engaged now. It didn't really matter what the content was, as long as they were really there in the community. And not just once or twice, but there for their whole college life.

Having spent most of my life working on the community side rather than the university side, another frustration was that the community had so little awareness of the resources that existed in the universities and colleges. I felt that if they could crack through the barriers, if they could really access and make use of the resources that the universities offer, it could be amazing. I was hoping we could figure out ways that the whole system here at the university could be made much more accessible to the neighborhood.

As Jane Addams School has evolved over the years, I've really seen the importance of certain ideas more and more. For example, amazing possibilities start to unfold when you see another person as a person, and not as something to be taught or fixed or served. You have to be with people just as who they are. When you see people as a role or as a static need, you limit what can occur. While I could say all of that before, it becomes real at Jane Addams School. I've seen the transformation of that idea into a reality on a daily basis.

A second one is public work. When we started, public work was still just a lot of words and a lot of going back to other people's history—like the CCC. But now we've got a multitude of examples where all of us at Jane Addams School have engaged in public work. I mean we haven't all done the same public work, but whether it's the citizenship group going to the Capitol or the Freedom Festival or the paj ntaub project, it just goes on and on. There are all these different things occurring, and when you collect all that and put it together—Wow!

We are realizing how strong and how important the doing of public work is. We are seeing how it changes the environment and the dynamic; it alters people's sense of who they are and what they can do. My understanding of this has gotten much stronger as I've stood back and looked at what we've been doing over the last two years. In the beginning it was more like, "Yeah, yeah, we've got to do this public work thing." But now we've got it, we're doing it.

The thing that has really surprised me, that I didn't anticipate in the beginning, is the intergenerational aspect of Jane Addams School. It leaps back and forth and in and out on a daily basis. Particularly my awareness of what happens for the kids as they're able to play multiple roles and as they're seen playing multiple roles. So sometimes they're the daughter of, sometimes they're the sister of, sometimes they're the person who teaches the dance group, sometimes they're the one who gives the speech at the governor's visit, sometimes they're the one who trains other people at another school, sometimes they're the people who do the translation for a small group of people. They play all these roles.

The opportunity to play these multiple roles that occurs for them through Jane Addams School ratchets up the experience for everybody, and it's particularly unique. I don't think there are other places where that occurs. What do they have in our society, in our town where people can come together to do things like this?

□

Growing up, I thought of freedom as something like being free of England in the Revolutionary War. We fought the war so we could be free of England. Or I related it to all the stories I heard about communism. There were all these things people weren't free to do in communist countries, but we were free to do them. We had freedom of speech and freedom of press. It was sort of something you had because somebody else got it for you. The American Revolution was fought; therefore, we are free. The slaves were freed by somebody else, so we don't have slavery anymore. Somebody did it, so freedom exists because somebody else did something along the way.

I've come to understand, though, that freedom is something that you do yourself. A big part of freedom is making the choice yourself; you have to do something. You liberate. Somebody else doesn't liberate you; you do the liberating. And you have to be constantly doing it. It's not a done deal. People have been in prison, and they have chosen freedom. And people have left prison, and they're still imprisoned. So there's something about it that has to be a constant act that you do.

What's always liberating for me is trying to create situations where people have the opportunity to liberate themselves, to make these choices. People have the capacity to do it, and they choose to do it, and somebody creates the opportunity and calls them forth to do it. The situation has to be there, but ultimately, the individual has to choose it. I think what we're doing at Jane Addams School is constantly creating the opportunity and the call for people to do more than they thought they could do, to practice their talents and to bring them forth. To the degree that we keep doing that, we really are about liberation and freedom. To the degree that we see freedom as static, we can imprison ourselves and each other.

JOYCE YAMAMOTO

Plua Hang Ly

Before I was married I helped my mother plant the garden, make rice and take care of my siblings—3 brothers and 6 sisters. When I was 7 years old, I could carry my baby brother. And by the time I was 10 years old, I could make a fire, cook rice, sweep the floor, feed the chickens, pig and goats. I was proud of what I could do.

Animals were a big part of our life, especially the rooster, who woke everyone at 4:00 in the morning. He was our only clock.

We had 10 dogs, and I always found time to play them. My parents kept the dogs to scare away the foxes from the chickens and the boys from sneaking in to see my sisters and me at night. Much later, when we had to leave Laos to go to Thailand, we tried to take one of our dogs with us, but he couldn't swim across the river, so we left him behind. My husband tied him to a tree at the river's edge. We could hear him crying for hours. It was very sad!

When I was 10 years old, I was big enough to carry the water. All the water in the village was put in a carve-out tree log. Everyone in the village came to the log to fill their bamboo tubes with water to take home. Every day we would go to the village water log to fill our bamboo tubes with water. We would put the bamboo in a basket to carry home on our backs. Each child would carry a basket that was the right size for them. Then, we would cut our wood for fire and the rice for food.

When I left Thailand for the United States, I carried my tools for cutting the rice and the wood and my basket for carrying water. The customs agents tried to take them away from me at the airport, but I wouldn't let them because I thought I would need them to heat my house and carry water. But when we got here life was easier. Houses had heat and gas stoves and the water came from a faucet.

But I still keep the tools that I carried all this way.

When I was 15 years old, the son of my mother's sister, Chua Xa Ly, lost his wife. They had six children, and one was just a baby. Chua lived north of us on the other side of the Mekong River, so it took him almost a year before he could travel south to my parent's village.

I became his wife and journeyed many days to his family's village.

My husband's mother taught me many things, because I was still like a child myself and didn't know how to sew, cook or take care of all the children. She died only five years later.

It was too soon.

Soon after that, the Communists came into Laos, destroying our villages. They knocked down our houses. They poisoned our wells and streams, so we had no water to drink. They dropped chemicals from the sky ("the yellow rain") which killed the pigs and chickens. The cows, horses and people lived for a while at least. Soon however, people also began to die from the chemicals. After two of my children had died, we fled to Thailand.

□

"On May 10, surrounded by Pathet Lao and North Vietnamese troops, with few surviving Hmong fighter pilots and no American combat support, Vang Pao reluctantly bowed to the counsel of his CIA officers and conceded that he could no longer hold Long Tieng. During the next four days, between 1,000 and 3,000 Hmong—mostly high-ranking army officers and their families...were airlifted by American planes to Thailand. (During the month before the fall of Saigon on April 30, 1975 American airlifts and sealifts had evacuated more than 45,000 South Vietnamese.) Hmong fought to board the aircraft. Several times the planes were so overloaded they could not take off, and dozens of people standing near the door had to be pushed out onto the airstrip. On May 14, Vang Pao, in tears, told the assembled crowd.

'Farewell, my brothers, I can do nothing more for you, I would only be a torment for you,' and boarded an evacuation helicopter. After the last American transport plane disappeared, more than 10,000 Hmong were left on the airfield, fully expecting more aircraft to return. When it became apparent that there would be no more planes, a collective wail rose from the crowd and echoed against the mountains. The shelling of Long Tieng began that afternoon. A long line of Hmong, carrying their children and old people, started to move across the plateau, heading toward Thailand."*

□

My husband's father, his second wife, son and daughter left our village first. One month later, my husband, his five children and I, pregnant, began our trek to Thailand. Along the way my husband found us temporary shelter in an abandoned village, because my son was ready to be born. He only lived for 10 minutes.

We waited for 10 days and then continued our journey.

We arrived in Thailand in 1975. Ten families from our clan joined us. During our four years there, my son Lau was born. He lived. Today, he, his wife and their two children live with us in St. Paul, Minnesota.

When we got to Thailand, there was no food. My family was so hungry. We were given only dry fish to eat. People became sick in their eyes from eating the fish–my eyes would water all night long. Ever since then I have had bad problems with my eyes. I can't read or drive. Sometimes they hurt so much that I cannot sleep at night.

One day, in 1979, a huge group of Hmong, Laotian and Cambodian people gathered at the refugee camp to listen to an American woman. She asked if we wanted to go to the United States. The group said yes, so we boarded buses and rode for five to seven hours until we came to airplanes that flew us to California and from there to Pennsylvania. We arrived in the United States in November 1979. My daughter Nicole was born in Pennsylvania the following September. A few months later, a bus took us to St. Paul, Minnesota.

I like it here, and I want to be a citizen. But it is very difficult because we have never been to school and we do not know English. We do not know the letters. When we go to the market, we do not know what to get. My father is 105 years old and my mother is 95 years old. They live in Laos. I think my mother has maybe two years left to live.

When I become a citizen, I will go to visit her. I worry that it will be too late.

---

* Anne Fadiman, The Spirit Catches You and You Fall Down. p.138.

JOYCE YAMAMOTO

Together: The telling of stories
Nan Skelton

Plua became a citizen on August 19, 1999. I was with her, along with Jennifer O'Donoghue, the day she passed her US citizenship test.

It was a beautiful sunny morning after a night of rain. Plua was dressed all in black. She gave Jennifer and me a cucumber from her garden, and then we drove with long silences as we struggled with our shared anxiety, and our simultaneous excitement:

What if she doesn't pass?

Soon she will pass!

The INS waiting room was filled with immigrants and refugees (from eight to ten different countries) waiting for their names to be called, seated in uncomfortable chairs pushed up against the walls like a doctor's office. Their eyes revealed their apprehension as they practiced the US government and history questions one more time. Others, too nervous to study anymore, spoke to their friend or spouse in hushed tones–the language of their birth countries. Beyond each person's private drama, made public by the INS office, there was nothing else to watch, to read or to distract; no magazines, no posters, no artwork, no books.

Nothing.

Shortly after Plua became a citizen she returned to Jane Addams School with her four youngest children (all born here in St. Paul) and announced that she and her children would continue coming to JAS.

She said, "My children need help with their school work and I need to learn to read. It will be hard but we will do it. Now that I have passed the citizenship test my head doesn't hurt so much and my eyes work better. It is not easy, but I will learn to read and so will my children."

Plua and I have ridden home together after JAS many, many times. During these times she has told me stories and taught me how to cook Hmong rice, what Hmong medicine to use for coughs and stomach aches, how to grow cilantro. She has told me her hopes and dreams for her children and for one day returning to Laos to visit her parents.

In a recent story she told in the car ride home from Jane Addams, she and western medicine met toe to toe. She had spent the night and long into the early morning hours at the hospital with her pregnant daughter-in-law. Apparently it is now common practice in the local hospital for older Hmong women to participate with their relatives in the birthing process. Plua was there, standing alert in the delivery room when the doctor decided because of his patient's rising blood pressure a c-section was necessary. Plua would not hear of it. She leapt into battle mode, moved her daughter-in-law onto her lap and began to massage the baby down the birth canal by rubbing her daughter-in-law's belly. Before long a healthy baby boy crowned and was born to the amazement of the physician and all but Plua.

Compared to American women her age, born here in the United States, Plua has lived through the equivalent of three to five generations. She moved from an agrarian, village clan, subsistence lifestyle, and oral culture to a 20th century urban lifestyle where she and members of her clan struggle to assume some of "what is America" without assimilating any further than they choose.

It means choosing literacy without losing the ability to listen to and respect Hmong elders; it means putting family and the clan before self or anything else; it means using things like modern plumbing and electricity but never forgetting "how we carried our water in Laos."

> "When you immigrate,
>   you become somebody else
>   from who you were." *

---

* Ursula Hegi, Tearing the Silence. p.140.

JOYCE YAMAMOTO

Cindy's Letter

Dear Mr. Senator,

Hello My Name is Cindy Xiong.
I am 10 years old and in 5th grade.
I'm here to talk about the citizen
test. My first concern is My parents.
My dad fail the citizen test. and
now I'm concern about My Mother.
She has been studing very hard
for the past year, I am still
sad that My father didn't pass.
I heard about some workers at
the INS office were unfair
they made the test harder than
it really should be. I was wondering
if you could please check there.

Thank you for your time.
        Sincerly,

            Cindy Xiong

A MESSAGE FROM THE PRESIDENT OF THE UNITED STATES

Victory at INS!

Jennifer L. O'Donoghue

On my way to pick up Koua I felt both excited and nervous. Feelings and thoughts spun through me as I drove to her house. How do I support Koua best? How can I be assertive with the INS people without jeopardizing Koua's goal of achieving her citizenship?

When I got to her house, her husband was busy cooking and washing dishes. Koua appeared, proudly wearing her JANE ADDAMS SCHOOL FOR DEMOCRACY T-shirt. On our way to the INS office, we chatted about feeling nervous, about her family, and about her eldest daughter whose husband is now living with his third wife. "He's no good for my daughter!" she said, adding that she wants them to get divorced.

Emblazoned on the INS building were official seals proclaiming "JUSTICE DEPARTMENT" and signs announcing that only "Those with scheduled interviews and their lawyers" were to be in the waiting room. We took a deep breath and walked in. The room was stark, windowless, intimidating. Filled with anxiety. Several other people sat waiting. Some sat alone, looking quietly ahead. Others were in small groups, heads down, speaking in hushed Vietnamese, Oromo, or Russian. There was no one to greet us, tell us what to do. But Koua had been here before and knew what to do. We placed Koua's appointment letter in the box on a table next to the door that lead to the examination rooms. Some time later, a faceless, bodiless hand reached out from behind the door and collected the letters.

As we sat there waiting, Koua studied her notes and asked me again and again to go over the difference between the governor and the mayor. We held hands, never letting go the entire time we waited.

After about twenty or thirty minutes, the door opened again, and a stern woman appeared. When she called Koua's name, I asked if I could go with her. "No," responded the examiner.

I was prepared for this response, but I had not figured out what my next move would be.

"Really? We were under the impression that these interviews are public and that unless Koua is against it, it's okay for me to be with her in the room," I said in my most polite voice.

The examiner responded curtly, "We don't do that."

I took a deep breath and gave her my ace in the hole. "Oh...well, we had a meeting with Curtis Aljetz* a few weeks ago, and he seemed to think that this shouldn't be a problem."

The examiner pursed her lips and said, "Let me go talk to my supervisor."

*Curtis Aljetz is the District Director of the Immigration and Naturalization Services.

[119]

For fifteen very nervous minutes, we waited. I was so afraid that I had messed things up for Koua.

The examiner came back and told me that I could accompany Koua for my "education" only. She was surprisingly nice to Koua, speaking slowly, repeating things, and working with her to help her understand. Koua, after nervously waiting for this moment, displayed no fear once in the exam room.

The exam room itself was set up so that there was a large and imposing desk between the examiner and examinee. Koua pushed this imposition aside, sitting down in the chair, leaning forward, and crossing her arms on the table as if to say, "Come on, give me your best shot!"

I almost laughed at how bold she was. She looked the examiner right in the eye. She emanated confidence and spirit. Koua is a woman filled with these qualities.

Throughout the exam, Koua spoke loudly and proudly. When the examiner asked if she had ever been involved in prostitution, Koua asked "What is prostitution?" After the examiner explained, Koua gave an indignant "No!" response. After many such questions from the application form, the examiner asked Koua 10 questions about government and history, of which Koua answered 7 correctly.* Ironically, one of the three she missed was about the mayor. She answered governor—her Achilles heel! Next Koua had to write "I have eight children," and then it was over.

She PASSED!!!

When we walked out of the interview room, we both simultaneously screamed and hugged each other.

Throughout the morning, our emotions had become so inextricably linked—our nervousness, excitement, joy, pride. Our response now was so natural. We turned to one another to celebrate what had become our success.

Suddenly, we became aware we were in the waiting room—many sets of eyes stared at us nervously. We hushed ourselves and hurried out of the room. Out in the parking lot, we continued our celebration. As we jumped up and down, screaming, with tears in our eyes, a group of Somali men standing nearby looked at us as if we were crazy. "She's a citizen!" I shouted to them. "Yeah!!" they responded in unison.

An instant connection was made around a common struggle.

On the ride home, we talked about our experience. Koua felt that my being in the room with her had made the examiner treat her with more respect and kindness than she had received on her previous visit to the INS. She also remarked that she felt less nervous with me there.

---

* The Citizenship Exam consists of questions relating to "moral character" ("Have you ever been a habitual drunkard?", "Have you ever been a member of the Communist Party?", "Have you ever been hospitalized with a mental illness?" and the like) and questions about the history and government of the United States.

[120]

I felt so honored that Koua would even want me to go with her, that she trusts me to be a part of such an important event in her life. I was glad to have been able to help her, even if it was just by sitting in the room with her. But I still worry about what this means.

Why should my presence make a difference in the way people treat immigrants? How can I be afforded more power than a mother of eight children who has risked her life to come to this country and struggles everyday to make a new life for herself and her family?

As we drove, we also made plans to share our experience publicly. We were both excited to bring our success back to everyone at the Jane Addams School. Koua felt that sharing her story with others was important because it would help them to feel less afraid. They would know that they could do it too. She had had difficulties, but she had struggled through them. She had won!

I realized how strong the Jane Addams School community has grown. Koua said that my presence made her feel more secure. I am sure that it was not just me, but what I represented—a community that loved and valued her, that would stand behind her and fight with her. We are engaged in a common struggle, and although each of us goes out and has different experiences, we know that others are behind us, and our victories are not complete unless we bring them back to share publicly with everyone.

JOYCE YAMAMOTO

Dear Representative

February 17,1998

Dear Representative,

My mom has been coming to the Jane Addams School to study for the citizenship test. She has been studying very hard the last several months. Can you try to do whatever you can to help her and others. THANK YOU!!!!

Sincerely ,
Mai Xiong

JOYCE YAMAMOTO

Nicole Ly

My dad's first wife died in Laos after they had five kids. My mom and dad were distant cousins. He was worried that his next wife wouldn't love his kids, so he and his family went to ask my mom's family if she would marry him. And she did.

But we don't really talk about that.

When I was younger, my mom told stories about the family, how they farmed in Laos, and then how they came to America. I remember the story of how they came to the United States because my mom would always say how they had to leave their black dog and two horses behind. They couldn't take the animals with them because they had to pay for every living thing they brought to America. They were really close to that dog.

It must have been hard for them.

Hmong people are really happy now, but America wasn't what they expected. I think they thought it would be easy to make money, that the roads would be paved with gold, so to speak; that kind of thing. Farming in Laos wasn't always easy for them. I can't speak for all Hmong people, but my family seems happy, even though they still talk about going back to visit Laos someday. I don't know how it was in Laos, but the elders always say that life in America is an easier way of life because people had to work so hard in Laos, even at a very young age. Everybody had to work on the farm. The younger kids had to go get the water for the day. People had it harder in Laos.

When coming to live in America, Hmong people experienced a lot of harassment, like racial slurs. My parents didn't know how to drive, so we would take the bus when we needed to get somewhere, and people used to stare at us.

My mom started going to Jane Addams School sometime last year. She would come home and often ask for help but then would forget everything at School the next time. She said they needed help with translation there, so one day I just went with her. I wanted to help my mom. I have been going to Jane Adams regularly ever since.

I depend on my parents, and Jane Addams School is an opportunity for me to give back. Initially, I worked with the adult circle. It gave me a break from screwing around. With the adults, it's serious work. I can tell that my mom feels closer to the college students she works with than I have with any of the teachers that I have ever had.

I remember in first grade, the teacher gave everyone a folder with a list of words. In the beginning, all the students started with the same list with three columns of words. In order to move on to the next level, you had to be able to read all those words. But the thing was, the teacher just gave it to us and expected us to know the words. Before the time I started school, I spoke Hmong. Probably the only English words I could say were "TV", "yes", and "no". In kindergarten all we did was artwork and singing songs; it was great but in first grade we needed to learn the alphabet and to read. It was harder for me. They didn't have any programs to help me. It wasn't until 3rd grade that I got into a program to help me catch up.

I used to get so frustrated.

When I was young, everything was so new, different, confusing. School was just one more thing to add to that list. In elementary school I was really, really shy. I didn't talk to the teacher that much. In every class, there was another Hmong student and I felt a little connection. We could speak Hmong together, and it made me feel confident; somebody was there who understood me.

I didn't feel that strange with the American students. In school, we were all kids, and they were just other kids that I could play with. There were little differences, but the cultural differences weren't a big deal. At home, in my neighborhood, it was different. My family didn't live in the best neighborhood. I learned to watch my back. In third grade, there was this bully who picked on me. Actually, he picked on everyone. But I thought he didn't like me because I looked different.

□

A lot of my values and beliefs come from my culture and family.

The family is really important in Hmong culture. If you have a problem you are supposed to go to the family first. For example, if you want to get divorced you have to go to the men of the family. I don't report all my problems to my family, but if I had problems at school I would go to my uncles. But it is getting to the point where it doesn't work anymore. My cousins wanted a divorce; they were nineteen years old. But the uncles didn't understand.

In Hmong culture, people are still old-fashioned.

My mom is always asking me when I am going to get married. When I do something wrong she says, "When you are married..." When I meet Hmong elders, the first things they ask me are, "Who are your parents?" and "Who are you married to?" Back in Laos, it was normal for thirteen or fourteen-year-olds to get married, but even now in America fifteen and sixteen-year-olds are getting married. I am not ready for getting married so young. I haven't really thought about it though. I guess if it happens, it happens.

My parents told me that in Laos, at age 13 or 14 you were treated as an adult. You were expected to stay at the farm overnight and tend to the work at early dawn. It was OK for them to marry so young because they already had responsibilities. That might have just carried over into America. In America when I was 12 or 13 years old I was babysitting, taking care of my sister's kids overnight when she had to work. But people around the neighborhood or at school who were not Hmong thought that was so odd.

It's just different expectations.

When I was younger I was tomboyish, and I had this aunt who was a lot like me. She has her BA in Psychology. We used to live in the same apartment building, so I guess I looked up to her. In the neighborhood, girls would be playing jump rope but I wouldn't know how to do it. I thought I was different. My aunt and her younger brother would come outside with baseball gloves and I would play with them.

> When I was younger, my parents kind of pressured me into staying Hmong.

They had me go to classes at church where I learned to read and write in Hmong. But the classes were fun, and I am really proud I know those things because many kids don't. I feel better knowing it because it is my culture. When I was younger, I felt pressure to speak only Hmong. Now, I don't know if my parents have changed or if I have been able to express myself better and explain to them that I wanted to speak English, too.

I think my parents are proud of me, but I've never really heard my dad talk about me. After I joined JROTC at Humboldt High School, I came home from school one day with my uniform on; my uncles were over at our house and recognized the army uniform. They asked my dad to explain what I was doing in a uniform. That was one of the first times I heard my dad tell people about me.

☐

Working at Jane Addams School has had a good effect on my life. I now look at my culture in a better way: I'm more proud to be Hmong. I'm interested in Hmong culture because others are interested. At home, it feels like my mom is lecturing me. At Jane Addams School, during the Cultural Exchange, others are talking. College students want to know about our culture. I learn a lot from the people and the cultural exchange time. Then I often go home and ask my mom more about these things and she explains them to me.

My mom tried to teach me how to sew paj ntaub when I was five, but I just gave up. When I was a kid I was more tomboyish. I didn't want to sit in the house sewing. Now I wish I knew how to sew because Hmong women are supposed to know that.

Hmong culture is not as much a part of my life as I'd like it to be. I feel more American. I haven't sat down to eat a traditional Hmong meal at all lately. But that is because I am so busy. I tell people I am very proud to be Hmong, but I might be a little bit more proud to be an American. I try to use English, but enough Hmong words so that my parents understand. I even think in English! To me, that's just normal.

> I am not as Hmong as I would like to be. I wish I could understand why some things are the way they are in Hmong culture. But I don't think I can.

People always assume I was born in Asia and are surprised when I say I was born in Philadelphia. Sometimes I feel bad about not being born in Laos or Thailand, and I feel less connected to my family history. I think this is an obstacle to my freedom in not being free to visit the place that my family came from.

> One of my goals is to go back to the house in Thailand where my family used to live. The atmosphere must be so different now.

JOYCE YAMAMOTO

The relationship between my generation and my parent's generation has drifted. When my parents meet other Hmong elders, even if they don't know them, they can talk. I feel like I don't want to talk to them. It's not cool. My parents can't really understand my generation. They think that if someone wears baggy jeans then he is automatically a gangster. Having college students and Humboldt students at Jane Addams School helps. When my mom met Jay at Jane Addams, who wore baggy pants, she said he was a good kid. This understanding comes as long as we have all kinds of people working together.

After school, I always look forward to coming to Jane Addams School. I've never done anything else where the whole family is learning together. Meeting the college students was the best thing. I got to hear stories about college, which eased my nerves. I also got to meet college professors and see what they are like.

If you had asked me what I was going to do this summer, I would have said I was just going to hang out. I never would have guessed I would be working on the farm with the children from Jane Addams School. It's nice for my cousins, too, because usually when I am babysitting them we can't do much. My cousins love it at the farm. They really like planting, and of course, swimming. It is a big adventure to them. They can always stay home and watch TV, but this gives them something productive to do. We are always trying to get all of our families together. We don't get to spend much time together, even at family parties. But there are four different branches of relatives that I go to the farm with. We get to spend time together there.

My mom is definitely not shy at Jane Addams School. Other places, when we talk to Americans, she needs a translator. But at Jane Addams School, she just walks in and starts talking. She doesn't hesitate. It's weird. When I am around my mom and Nan, she usually asks me to interpret. But when she and Nan are alone, they just talk. Confidence might have something to do with it. Maybe she feels uncomfortable speaking English around us, her children.

I think the Hmong elders are moving towards a greater understanding of freedom in the United States. Being a citizen will allow my parents to be accepted and free. It is the feeling of being free that comes from being a citizen. Having the feeling of being able to say, "Yes, I can vote."

Judy Ly

One day when I was about five years old, I asked my mom where we came from because I noticed that we were different than the other kids in my class. She told me that we were from Laos.

As I got older, I learned more about our Hmong history. In sixth grade, we were assigned a project in which we had to ask our parents about where we came from and why we came to America.

My mother told me that we lived in a town in Laos called "54" (in Hmong). It was during the Vietnam War that we decided to go to America because of the fighting in Laos.

There was a secret war going on because the United States told the Hmong people that if a boy was over the age of ten, he had to help the Americans fight against the Vietnamese. In 1975, my parents and brothers crossed the Mekong River into Thailand. They were able to use a big boat to cross the river since they were some of the first people to cross that night. The people that came after them had to use canoes, and the people after that had to find their own way across, usually by swimming.

My family was not able to take anything with them, and they had to leave even their horses and dogs. My mother was pregnant at the time of the journey, but because of the pollution from the war, the baby died soon after birth.* Everyone in my family got split up once they reached Thailand, but somehow they met up later in a refugee camp. A couple months after that, they flew to the United States.

My mom doesn't usually talk much about all this. If we ask a bunch of questions then she'll tell us things, but usually she tells us it is in the past, and never mind about it. There are a lot of things that happened to her that she wants to keep to herself and if so, I should accept her wishes.

When I was younger, it didn't seem like kids cared about differences. But when I entered school all that changed. Starting when I was in kindergarten, the kids treated me differently because of where I was from and my skin color, religion, the way I dressed, and the way I spoke. I didn't speak much English.

I remember this one time at school when I left my jacket outside in the winter. I couldn't say "jacket" in English, so I got really mad and yelled in Hmong. My teacher didn't understand. Finally she realized that my jacket was outside and she let me go and get it, but I was still so confused. I was furious that she hadn't understood what I had said. I needed my jacket and she didn't understand.

Even now in high school there are groups of Hmong, Cambodians, African Americans, and Caucasians. There are only a few groups that have a mix of kids. I don't know why that is but I think it is just because of our skin color. I have friends that are Hmong and American and whatever. I don't like that people don't like people just because of their different skin color.

> I am Hmong because I speak Hmong,
> but then again, I speak English.
> Being Asian is in my blood.
> I think I act more like I am American

---

* "Pollution" here is used to refer to the chemical weapons used during and after the war. For more information, see Jane Hamilton-Merritt's Tragic Mountains.

but sometimes I act like I am Hmong,
only I don't speak Hmong that much.
I don't dress "Hmong" to school,
just in jeans and t-shirts.
I know and understand Hmong,
but I can't write it.
Mostly, I feel like myself.
I don't feel American all of the time,
nor do I feel Hmong all the time.
I guess my self is Hmong.

One part of being Hmong is that you have more chores than regular American kids do. Hmong kids' chores are making rice (which takes an hour or so), cooking meals (especially when your parents are sick), cleaning the bathroom, bedrooms, and the living room so that nothing is on the floor. In Hmong households, people walk around with bare feet. So we have to vacuum once a day.

Another way I am Hmong is that I still eat rice, and that is part of the Hmong culture. When I dress in traditional Hmong clothes and go to Hmong celebrations and events, that proves I am still Hmong. But I think I am more American because I would rather have pizza over rice. And I don't wear Hmong dress to school everyday. Everybody would stare at me if I did, and I wouldn't want to anyway.

I go to Hmong celebrations because some of them are fun, and you get to meet new people. Sometimes people other than Hmong people go, too. At the Hmong festivals I notice that there is not just one kind of Hmong. For example, there are Chinese-Hmong, Black Hmong, White Hmong, and Green Hmong. The dresses that people wear look different, too.*

I have a problem when people say "Go get into your Hmong costume" at the festivals because I don't believe it is a costume. I think it is just plain clothes. If you think it is a costume then right now I would be wearing a costume too, in my jeans and t-shirt, because that is what people wear here. We shouldn't say costume just because it was what was worn in Laos everyday. I think people should say, "Change into your clothes."

Hmong people think that if you have a daughter, she is a guest in the family. When she gets married, it is not like the husband's family says, "Oh, you came."* They say, "Welcome. You are home." Your family is more connected with their sons than their daughters because of this. My mom connects with everyone. My dad doesn't know how to show emotions or feelings. My mom is the one who lectures us on life. Dad is the one on the side saying, "YAH". We know they love us the same, but my mom just shows us she loves us more.

* These designations represent different "strands" of Hmong experience. While these "strands" cut across clans, each has a distinct dialect and style of dress. "Strands" named by a color refer to the clothing worn by the women.
* "Koj tuaj, los," directly translated as "Oh, you came," is the traditional Hmong greeting for someone who is a visitor to their house.

I don't talk to my dad much because daughters and fathers don't connect as well as the mother and sons. I think it is because the sons are going to carry on the last name and the woman is not. If you are a woman, you lose both your names in some cases because Hmong people refer to you as "so and so's wife". I think it is a waste to give a woman any name then, because you have both of them changed when you are married anyway.

What's the point?

When I get married I am keeping my name—Judy Ly—because my parents gave me that name. But if anyone asks me whose wife I am, I will say,

"My name is Judy Ly, but I am married to so and so."

I don't know about other Hmong people but when my boyfriend, Tang, comes over I am supposed to stay in the house, in the same room as everyone else in my family. If we do leave the house, someone, like my brother or sister, has to come with us, even on a walk. I feel like my privacy has been taken away. But we can go out with friends, so if my boyfriend and I go in a group then it is OK.

I don't know about marriage laws in Laos because technically Hmong men could have more than one wife. But the way I look at it, Hmong marriage doesn't work out for me. I don't like the way it is. I would go for an American marriage if I could.

There is a saying in Hmong culture that as soon as you say "I DO" you are not allowed to look back, and can only look straight ahead into the future. They say your future will be destroyed if you look back. Some people say their good-bye's before the wedding and never look back into their past for fear their future will be bad.

When I get married, I want my lifestyle to be American. But I don't really know how an American lifestyle or marriage is, because I live in a Hmong house. I think American marriage is less painful. For example, if my husband wanted to have a second wife, Hmong people would be like, "Oh, go for it." I don't think Americans would be like that. But I don't want to marry an *American* American. I want to marry a Hmong who understands his background, but that he lives in America now.

I want to teach my kids to make rice three times a day. My mom taught me how to make rice. First I watched a couple of times, and then she talked me through making the rice. I was in the first grade.

As far as high school goes, I just want to graduate. I want to prove to myself and to my mom that I can do it. It would be very different in Laos. I would be home sewing and cooking and my brother would be off to school, except if we were poor. Then my brother would have to stay home, too.

I admire my mom because she is courageous. She has been here twenty years. She left her mom in Laos and hasn't seen her since. Despite this, she never says how sad she is because of that or yells at us because she misses her mom. I don't know my grandma at all. After wondering about my grandma, I just forgot about her. She is so old now and still in Laos. We have to send her tapes of us talking since she can't read or write. She just knows her grandchildren's names. She doesn't know what we look like. I've never seen a picture of her either. My mom talks about her a lot though, and how she wants to go to Laos to see her before she dies.

Update: 1 year later, after Judy's marriage to Tang in the summer of 1998 at age 16...

Usually what happens with Hmong marriages is the man goes to the woman's house with his father or the family "judges" and they ask the father, not the woman, if he can marry her. But with a lot of marriages, the woman just leaves with the man and her family can't take her back. If she is not emotionally strong enough she'll have to go back to her family. But if she is strong enough, she'll get married.

I left with Tang on a Monday. Two Sundays later we had the wedding. My mom was kind of mad at me because I was so young. My brother got married at a very young age. It caused her a lot of stress that I didn't wait either. The day after I stayed with Tang and his family, my mom kept asking me to come home, but I wouldn't. She cried out, "You don't want to cook and clean for me anymore. That's why you left." I feel bad it was so hard for my mom when I got married. She lost a lot of hair because of me.

I thought that when I got married everything was going to be better. My mom wouldn't be able to yell at me anymore, and I would be able to go to places I was never able to go to before. But now I miss my mom yelling at me, and I do go to different places, but it is just not how I pictured it. I sometimes regret getting married so young. But really, our marriage is good. All couples have problems and arguments, but they work it out.

Now that I am married, I miss hanging out with my friends. When you are married you can't do that whenever you want. Plus, I don't know how to cook and clean. You really should master these things before you get married because your life would be so much better if you could do those things. Then your husband could just sit down and relax. He goes to work and in return you cook and clean for him.

Some people say women shouldn't be locked in a house cooking and cleaning, but I think that if a husband works for both of you, then why not cook for him to please him? He's pleasing you. But he also has to let you have your own life, so you can visit your family and friends, and do the things you want to. Tang goes to work and I cook and clean for him. But he lets me go to Jane Addams School, and I can go to my parents' house any time I want. He lets me have my own time.

It is customary for a Hmong bride to receive an outfit from the family. When Tang and I first got married, I was given a new outfit. One day Tang and I went to the laundromat. I brought bleach and put it in the two loads of whites we had. Later, Tang asked me whether I had put detergent in the rest of the loads, and proceeded to pour the bleach in all the loads. I started yelling, "Why did you do that?" We ended up having to buy new clothes, and I didn't let him do the wash for a while.

What I have noticed at the laundromat is that usually the Hmong husbands just sit and don't do anything while their wives do all the work. But Tang helps me. Even after three years of being together, he helps. He tells me to go do my homework while he washes the clothes. Then we have an argument about who gets to do the laundry.

Tang's parents live with us but they mostly take care of themselves.

They stay with Tang's brother some nights, too. I guess you can say that they watch our house for us while I am at school and Tang is at work. I don't cook and clean for them as much as they do for me. They know I am in school so they often do things for me. I don't have time to see my family and friends so much anymore. I see them about once a week, or whenever I feel the need. I sometimes talk to my mom on the phone, but that is usually because she wants me to help out with my younger brother. I don't just call her up to talk about my day.

Tang understands the Hmong background. It seems that American people have their own lives, and both of us have something that is just our own. But still, for the rest of my life, some people are not going to call me Judy Ly. They are going to call me Tang's wife. When I said last year that I think it is a waste to give a girl a name because of this, I guess I just feel it is too bad that women are not known by their name throughout their whole life.

My older sister, Nicole, left for college last summer—the summer I got married. At first I didn't want her to go to college so far away. During that summer especially, I worried about who would help out at home since we both would not be there. But I just kind of accepted Nicole leaving because it was what she wanted to do. Before she left we would fight a lot, but now I miss talking to her. I ask her, "When are you going to come home?"

I haven't really thought about my future. I think about what to do for dinner or when my husband is going to go to sleep so I can watch T.V. Life is better if you just let it happen instead of trying to plan it all out.

Tang and I talk about the names our kids will have. I want a boy and a girl. Now I am in school though, so I don't have time for a kid. And if I go to college, I wouldn't have time either. I do think about college, but I would not live in the dorms so I could be with Tang. After I graduate from college, there is always work. It seems like there is no time in life for children.

I like to work at Jane Addams School. My sister says, "Who says there has to be a reason to volunteer?" It makes me feel good and it makes the other people feel good. It is a win-win situation. Working in the Children's Circle makes the time go faster, and I am much better at working with kids. I learn a lot of things from the kids—little bits about life that teenagers don't think about. In the kids' eyes you are a leader. They follow you.

My experience at Jane Addams School is important to me for many reasons. I want to know what to do with my own kids someday. I also need opportunities to be with adults. At Jane Addams School I interact with both kids and adults.

D'Ann Urbaniak Lesch

Home: Mirror Twins, Mirror Houses

I was born on April 15, 1973. Tax deduction day; that's what the birth
announcement read. I was followed ten minutes later by my twin sister.
Mirror Identical Twins. I was left-handed and she was right-handed.
And as far as bald-headed crying babies go, we looked the same.
Except I had a huge mole—though growing up I referred to it as a
"birth mark" because I thought it sounded better—on my forehead.
That became the way to tell D'Ann Lynn and Cheryl Lee apart.

I grew up in Minneapolis, and lived in the same house all my life—until college. It was a "double bungalow—two houses side by side," and I explained it just like that to anyone who asked me. The people who lived in the other side of the house were my best friends, the Maurelli's. The doorways of both families' kitchens opened up into a shared hallway, basement, and door to our backyard. Growing up in such close proximity and relationship to another family was a really unique experience; but at the same time, it was a part of my childhood and who I was, so it didn't seem that unusual to me then.

In my family, there was me and Cheryl, my younger brother David, and my mom and dad. In the Maurelli family, there was Gino, who was our age, Erin, two years older, and Peter, who was 4 years older. When people asked me who my brothers and sisters were I always wanted to include Peter, Gino, and Erin. I don't think people understood why. But I knew. We all did.

My father is 100% Polish, and grew up in Cicero, a Polish suburb of Chicago. His father changed the family name to "Urban" for most of my father's childhood, I think because of the stigmas attached to being too "ethnic" and seemingly "un-American." My mother grew up on a farm in Western Minnesota and is a mixture of Norwegian, Swedish, and German. My "other parents," Joe and Judy Maurelli, grew up in different environments too; Joe's family being from Italy, and Judy was Polish and raised in North Minneapolis. There were differences in the way each couple raised their children, but they treated us all like we were their kids.

Our families went to the same church, and I think that's how my parents and Joe and Judy ended up moving in together. I never really understood how they ended up buying a house together—maybe to save money. They looked in the suburbs, but people in the suburbs thought they were crazy hippies and wouldn't let them do it. So they found this place in Minneapolis. My family has been there ever since. The Maurelli's moved to another house when I was in 6th grade.

Being a twin has been so much fun.

Cheryl and I grew to know each other so well, that it does feel eerie sometimes. We always had each other to play with, tell secrets to, and give each other back rubs late at night in the lower half of the bunk bed. Even now, I know she is always there for me, will support me, and be my best friend no matter how much I annoy her some days. And our relationship has gone through major changes, the most recent one being both of us getting married. (No, we did not have a double wedding, but yes, I know that would've been so cute!) It's amazing to look back over all the changes and realize how she and I have grown together—and loved each other through all of it.

Being a twin has been bittersweet.

When we were little—and even now to some degree—we looked a lot alike. We both had to deal with people saying, "Which one are you?" or "Those are the twins." It is something I've had to work through, to find my own space in the world. I think I spent a lot of my life building my identity outside the status of being a twin. In high school I grew out my bangs, finally allowing my birthmark to be shown. All through childhood, since it was the easiest way to tell Cheryl and I apart, people would lift our bangs and say, "Oh, you're ____." It played such a role in defining me, that I chose to cover it—for a long time.

Family Time, Music, and Pizza

When I was growing up, we did things as a family. It was important to spend time together. Every summer we all looked forward to driving to Pennsylvania to a church convention. We went to family camp together. My dad was a teacher and didn't work summers, and my mother worked part time and got summers off. They were home a lot. We always had dinner as a family. We had a family tradition where we prayed before every meal and before bedtime. And whoever set the table got to pick who prayed, so it was kind of a fun thing to set the table because then you got to nail anyone who you wanted to make pray.

Another tradition was music. We had a piano, and my dad plays. Sometimes before dinner my dad would start playing from the church hymnal, and my sister and I would run down the stairs and sit on opposite sides of him. He would play and we would sinG. We'd quickly page through the hymnal after he finished a song and pick another we wanted to sing. That was always a really soothing and spiritual time for me to be able to sit and sing. The smells of dinner drifted from the kitchen into the living room air, and I could hear my mother banging on pots. The "cook's helper," one of the chores we chose from each week, would head in to help her, and soon "TIME TO EEE-EAT" would be shouted out over the music.

Thursday was pizza night at the Urbaniak house. My mom made the whole-wheat pizza crust, and my dad put together the toppings. All of us kids helped out in the kitchen too, with grating the cheese and other assigned tasks. I think growing up with so many moments like those is why I like doing things with people so much. Whether it's cooking or walking or whatever, I like experiencing things with people I love.

Moving Out

Leaving home was a big step for me.

But I was ready by the time college rolled around. I packed my bags and boxes and headed on my way—with my parents' calling card in hand. It was hard to leave my sister, but we talked and wrote at least once a week.

I studied sociology in college; I loved learning different ways of seeing people and why things are the way they are. I wanted to go to graduate school right away so I could teach Sociology, but something held me back. I needed to experience more. I wanted to live abroad—in a culture that was different from America.

So I left for Japan and lived there for two years teaching English. It was the first time I had lived on my own, not to mention abroad. I didn't know anybody, and I didn't speak the language. I couldn't read anything in Japanese. I couldn't understand anything.

It taught me a lot about people, and a lot about myself. I am the type of person who likes to know what's going on, what's going to happen. In Japan I only understood a little of what was going on around me. As much as I asked people and got translations, things never happened the way I pictured. I remember my first day walking into the school, being led into the front office. I had to sit and drink green tea, use my hanko (a Japanese name stamp) to sign forms, bow to everyone I met and give them little presents from America—and I didn't understand anything that was going on.

I had to learn to let things happen and trust that it would be OK.

It was hard and scary. Everything I did felt like a courageous act, from speaking Japanese to another teacher who didn't speak English, to using formal Japanese to the principal, who I needed to address differently because of his position. At the same time, I was myself. I think that impacted a lot of people. I was the only Westerner at the Japanese all-girls high school where I worked. I was watched, and I knew it.

I also learned about different ways to communicate with people, to express my self and my feelings in ways other than words.

There was a teacher named Hanesaka-sensei. Everyday at lunchtime, she would sit at her desk and peel and cut a huge red apple. Then she would give me a piece. Always. We shared her apple everyday. On my last day at the school, after the graduation ceremony where I gave my farewell speech in Japanese, we huddled together in the principal's meeting room. It would be our last time together for a long time. She peeled and cut her apple and shared it with me. And we cried.

Sense of Family, Community, Love, and God

I was brought up so that my immediate family relationships and my connections to other people were (and still are) of utmost importance.

That's why when I started dating a friend from college, I knew it was special. Jim and I put the emphasis on our friendship first—which in some ways was easier to do considering I was in Japan and he was in Iowa. Over the course of time, our relationship deepened; from letters, emails, and phone calls we got to know each other better than if we had been living next door. When I did come back to America and we both were living in Minneapolis, it was like putting in the final piece of the puzzle. We got engaged within six months, and were married later that year.

I hope that when Jim and I have children they will feel strength from our family. I hope that we will all continue to appreciate and learn from the differences and similarities in many families. And together, we will be part of a larger community, whether it be our extended families, neighborhood community, or church community.

I've learned a lot from my family. My dad never talked badly about people. He never came home from work and said things about people in a bad way. If he had ill feelings toward people, he seemed to be proactive rather than putting people down. Whenever I visited his work, people would tell me that he was well respected.

"Your dad is so great. He is such a good man. "

Also important to pass on to my children is a sense of having God in our lives. Being from a different religious background from Jim, I am aware that we must figure out a way to work together to help our children see and feel God in their everyday lives. It will be our challenge to model ways for our children to trust in us and trust in God.

Faith in God has played a huge role in my life. I think the first time I really felt that I could indeed trust in something that I couldn't "see" was when I went to Japan. I remember when I left I said "I'll just wait and see how it goes." I didn't know how living there would change the way I chose to practice my faith. But when I got there I met the most amazing Christian people, and I saw that as a sign that no matter where I go or what I do, God is with me. Faith just exists, and it is up to me to believe.

So now when I get concerned about some things working out, I remind myself to look at it in a larger context, to remember that God has a hand in this, too; to trust Him. This is work for me and it takes connection, just like connecting to people. It takes time and effort to be the person I want to be.

Faced with "Freedom"

It is hard for me to talk about what freedom means. It has so many different layers. Growing up, I didn't think about what freedom meant because I hadn't had a situation where the lack of freedom stared me in the face.

I had this experience when I went to Vietnam in 1996.

I was traveling with some friends in Da Nang, which is near China Beach. We were there over Christmas and decided to go to church on Christmas Eve. We went to this outside service in a huge cement yard, kind of like a playground. It was fenced in and packed with hundreds of people. There was a stage in the front with a play going on—though I wasn't sure the connection of the play to Christmas since I didn't speak Vietnamese. At the end, all of a sudden we heard these loud noises. There were armored trucks filled with men coming our way.

"What's going on? Where are they going?

Instead of going to the "trouble," they were circling us. The Vietnamese woman we were with turned to us and said, "They're circling because they think there is going to be a revolution. They're scared that all these people might revolt. Every year this happens. They circle the Christmas mass."

At that moment it dawned on me what it felt like not to have free-dom—freedom of religion in this case.

The feelings I experienced there still haunt me. Crowds of people, the noise of the armored cars, men with helmets and guns afraid of people who were trying to celebrate their religion together. I think that was the first time I was consciously thankful for the freedoms I have in America.

When I told my father this story, he told me that my grandparents came to America to have freedom of religion; that was so important to them and just as important to us. My father was a conscientious objec-tor, and wouldn't fight in the Vietnam War. But at the same time, he has served his country in many ways.

Knowing all the families and hearing the stories of my Hmong friends at Jane Addams School, how they escaped from Laos to Thailand, has had a big impact on my life. I see the need to really know those struggles. But at the same time, I need to know my own family's struggles and their stories of coming to America. But I don't.

With my own extended family, so many things get in the way. It is not easy pulling them aside, asking them to tell stories about their life. I've done that a few times with my grandma, who has been without her husband for a long time. It's hard to do. People don't ask her enough, if at all. What do you do when someone says,

> "Tell me about your life."

When you've lived a full life of experiences, where do you start?

Citizenship, Learning, and Magic

My father chose—because of his beliefs—not to fight in the Vietnam War. I'm very proud of him for acting on his beliefs and not fighting. Hmong people fought in the war for what should have been theirs in the first place: their lives, their freedom, their land, their way of life. My father had a choice not to fight and still have his freedom. But the Hmong people didn't have that choice. They had to fight to survive. So they did. Eventually, they had to escape the fighting in order to survive.

A lot of Hmong men fought in the Vietnam War. They fought with America because of what they believed in. I can imagine that being very frustrating, knowing you risked your life and family and ultimately had to leave your country for freedom. Only to have the government stance in America be "You can't have your citizenship because you weren't born in this country. You fought with us, but we covered it up and ordi-nary people don't know about it. So now you have to earn citizenship."

I get frustrated with the citizenship questions on the test, because the questions don't hold as much meaning as what we experience together, studying each day. Just seeing people come back every Monday and Wednesday to study, to improve their English and work side-by-side with all of us is a lesson in determination that shows me how important it is for them to become U.S. citizens. Their strength helps me to look at what citizenship and freedom mean to me.

In my second month at Jane Addams I was working with Bee Lee, an older, delightfully funny woman. We went in the hall because we were frustrated with all the noise in the crowded room where everyone was working. For an hour and a half, I tried to make visual the three branches of government. I taped paper up on the brick wall to try to get my points across. Bee Lee and I would communicate in whatever way worked at the moment. Sometimes it was in the form of gesturing, smiling, basic sentences. But however we did it, we had fun! At the end of the night, I remember she turned to me and said she liked working with me because she "learned a little". At first I thought, "Oh no, she only learned a little." But I learned with time, that to her, a little was a good thing.

I love being around Jane Addams because it's a true community, where kids are running around with their parents. I said once during a cultural exchange that I get more hugs in one night of "Jane Addams time" than 6 months of "regular time." It means so much to me to feel

JOYCE YAMAMOTO

[147]

that the kids love and know me and care that I'm there. I think our cultural exchanges—real discussions about what's important to people and the experiences they're having—helps everyone think through where they are at. This last year at Jane Addams I've been more reflective than I ever have been. I've been able to talk through what's been happening to me, what I've learned and what I've done. I don't know what I'll do with the rest of my life, but I hope I'll always have a chance to reflect with the people around me, to learn from what we are experiencing.

The magic about Jane Addams is that it is invented as it goes, by different people. It's not just this place. It's this thing that grows depending on how many people give it attention and support—sort of like a bed of flowers. It grows by different people coming in and being a part of it and owning it saying, "This is mine. This is part of me."

There isn't a set road that Jane Addams needs to take, but as a group we can plunge ahead while realizing there isn't a place we have to get to. If there was a place we had to get to, like the citizenship test, then Jane Addams School would end. But because of its organic nature, it will keep re-inventing itself.

There is always more we can learn from each other.

"Freedom is the collective ability to shape our lives together."

Nan Kari

Section 5
Sandy Fuller
Susie Chang*
Seng Yang
Nan Kari

JOYCE YAMAMOTO

Sandy Fuller

A struggle that I had to fight the hardest to overcome was that I was basically tongue-tied at birth and it was not corrected until I was seven. Since you form the basic speech patterns by the time you are three and learn how to swallow and use your facial muscles in the first two months of life, I developed these differently than others, none of which, to this day, I do the way everyone else does. I was a student in college when I could finally make someone understand me the first time they asked what my name was.

I spent most of my childhood with this inability to be understood by other people. It didn't stop me from trying to talk; but nobody knew what I was saying, except for a few people. This is when I got my first taste of, and my first interest in, the whole arena of discrimination. I was told repeatedly that I couldn't do anything. I was told I couldn't go to college, have an academic diploma, told that I couldn't learn a foreign language.

> Needless to say, I don't believe it when people say I can't do something.

> What I tell people now is, if you tell me it's impossible, that just means it takes a little longer to do it, that's all.

I grew up in a rural area, and my family produced most of our own food. We were a poor family. Later in life, my idea of working with people who are poor, and being concerned about the perceptions of people who are poor probably grew out of that.

I grew up in a house where foster children were a part of the household, and we considered them a part of the family. There were many friends and relatives that couldn't tell which kids were foster kids and which kids, as they would put it, "belonged". We'd get very frustrated and say, "All of us".

> I was the first one in my family to go to college. Actually, I was the only one in my generation. I have about 40 first cousins.

I came out of an area that has a very strong Germanic tradition. There are things I can't buy here in Minnesota, like food, which I grew up with. The names are different here too. People here don't have any of the names I knew back home. Whether you're German or not, if you come out of that area, you're Germanic. In terms of my actual heritage, I have a little bit of German heritage; very small compared to the impact of growing up in a highly German area.

□

I'm from Maryland, and grew up on the Maryland/Pennsylvania state line. When I was in school in the late 50's, integration became an issue.

> But to a lot of people my age, it was obvious that in Maryland segregation was a fact of life.

I didn't go to an integrated school till I was in 9th grade. There were people in my classes who were part of the group I hung out with, but they were not accepted in other groups because of their color. Those school experiences definitely had an impact on me. It also had an impact that many of our parents would not allow us, as a group, to be in their homes. We couldn't go to my house as a group. There ended up being only one place we could be at because most of the parents couldn't deal with us being an interracial group of kids.

When I got into college and started working at camps, kids were just starting to integrate more. I was asked if I would consider rooming with an African-American staff member, the only African-American on staff. They were looking for someone who would be willing to share accommodations. I said yes.

In the early to mid 60's, I got involved in issues of how people were treated because of their race. My friends and I experienced things like leaving camp to go get an ice cream cone, and instead being told we couldn't get served. We had to make special efforts to go places we knew served both blacks and whites. We watched tables of all blacks or all whites being served, but we had to just sit there. Nobody acknowledged our existence for hours, because of our mixed group.

> We didn't go to practice civic disobedience—we went because we just wanted something to eat! Very simple kinds of things like that got me more involved with working cross-culturally.

I came to Minnesota at the end of the 70's to run a camp. We did things that brought Asian kids into camp, and hearing impaired kids into camp. We had staff members who signed. We had all the campers thinking the motions to the songs were sign language because every song had motions so everyone could participate. We experimented with a variety of issues where people would say, "This person can't do that!" and we'd say, "Well, maybe they can. Let's figure out how." Some things were successful, but some we would have to say, "This isn't working." We needed to learn more before we tried it again.

From there I got a job to run camps for Neighborhood House. I was told that Neighborhood House was about serving the West Side community, but it had a camp that the kids from the West Side didn't go to. Instead, kids from all over the city that had the money to go to camp went. So we all talked about the finances and about what people wanted the camp to be. By the next summer, 95% of the kids attending it were West Siders. That meant we had to be attuned to issues that were important to the West Side community. We went into a day camp program but structured it like a resident camp. Initially, I had trouble finding counselors who looked like the kids that we served, so we found ways to hire high school students to work with college students as a team. They both played different roles in leadership, and each team reflected the kids from the community. That job got me into Neighborhood House, and in 1986, a year and half later, I became the Program Manager.

□

In 1996, when we started planning Jane Addams School, some people said, you cannot work together unless you put together some sort of structure. But we were working on a looser model that said if we agree on something and can stay focused on the mission, then the structure will work itself out.

JOYCE YAMAMOTO

Jane Addams School was built on the idea of working in collaborations, not wasting energy in putting together some super-structure. Yes, it's messy for some folks but that messiness also gives us the strength to be responsive. We wouldn't have been able to do that if we had made a lot of rules. And it's worked out—even though we struggle sometimes and always will. But it's important that people buy into that mission.

Being responsive to those things that were identified by West Side residents was a philosophy people were talking about that felt more comfortable than what we often hear from institutions. It was a philosophy that said that there are things that we can learn from the community: that we don't have all the answers for the community.

When we started Jane Addams School, I wasn't sure what we were doing, but I figured that somehow we would be helping residents to address needs that they had. People would not be saying, "We know you need this". Rather, "What is it that you would like?" "What is it you can share with us as we help you work on the things that are important to you?"

> People in the community receive something out of that exchange and at the same time they are treated in a respectful manner and have an opportunity to contribute.

This idea is difficult for people because I don't think we often ask them to give, and that's a hard concept to get across—the idea that we're here to help them, but at the same time who says they can't help themselves? I think there is a craziness involved: "Well, they obviously need my help, so I have to do this for them!" instead of, "How do we help people do this for themselves?" And finally, how do we make it accessible? Don't tell me it's accessible because somebody else did it. It may not be accessible to everyone. The question has to be, how do we make it accessible, not how do we do it for them!

□

The citizenship element has helped Jane Addams School. It has given people something to focus on. It has given us a common bond. The citizenship issue was a godsend in getting us off the ground in the Hmong Circle. I think it will be interesting to see how we evolve with the Hmong Circle as people achieve their citizenship and we try to move into other topics. I am not sure what that is going to look like.

> A major breakthrough for me in understanding all that Jane Addams School could do was when Seng Yang told us about his sister reading the newspaper to him.

Seng had been very adamant about having a teacher for her. The "everyone's a teacher, everyone's a learner" didn't fit into his knowledge of how things worked in the world. But then he came in and reported that about his sister being able to read to him—that her efforts in studying for the citizenship test at Jane Addams had helped her learn other things as well.

One of the neat things about Jane Addams School is the persistence and determination that we see from people who are working so hard to become a part of a society that is so different from anything they have ever known. At the same time, one of the frustrating things is some of the ways people respond to immigrants, or people who are "unknown". The put downs, the "Oh, if they wanted to work they could." "Oh, they are just lazy."

I don't see laziness. I have never seen laziness. I have never seen anything but a true desire to create a world in which their kids can be successful, whether or not they get to grasp that for themselves isn't even as relevant. I look at families who we deal with day in and day out here at Neighborhood House and I hear constantly what people want for their kids. It is a very positive thing that they are trying to work for.

As someone who has always had freedom, I think I always assume it. It tends not to be a concept I think about. I have an appreciation about what people have gone through for the privilege of being part of this culture; that through things like civil rights, people can be respected for what they have to offer, instead of cast aside for how they are different. That has continually been an issue that has been important to me, a big issue I tend to focus on.

> How do we ensure that all of us are respected for who we are and what we have to contribute; instead of being told what we cannot do, or what we won't be allowed to do?

PETER LEACH

Susie Chang*

---

* The name Susie Chang is a pseudonym.

Freedom is doing what you want...

Not being controlled.

For example, in Laos, you could build a house wherever you wanted, you could farm wherever you wanted; no taxes, no government looking over your shoulder. The Hmong people in Laos didn't work for other people.

Freedom means being with your friends and family...
Wherever your rice field was was where you belonged, you and your family.

In my parents' generation, they didn't have anything. I mean, everything was free as long as you worked hard for it. You should have been able to make it from day to day.

But during the war and after the war, the Communists controlled everything. Because of the war, we belonged to the Communists. Whatever we made became theirs.

It was so hard.

□

In America, being a woman, you can go to school. You can get an education and maybe go on to college. You can have a good job; a better job than even a man can get.

In Laos, little girls were taught that they had to stay home, to cook and clean for their parents and brothers. All they did from morning till night was work. And if a family was lucky enough to have a son, he would go to school, but a girl was not allowed to go to school and get an education.

In Laos, that's what we were taught. That was the way, generation after generation.

In America, it's better. Girls can do just as much as boys can.

□

To imagine Laos, picture a big mountain...

Most people lived in clans. One town on the mountain would be the Ly clan, the next town would be the Vang clan, and so on.

Before planting, a man would go and look for a particular spot, and he would say,

"Oh, this looks like a good spot, with good soil."

He would mark it by chopping down a tree so other people would know someone had been there already. People respected that; there was no fighting over it. If people didn't respect that, then they would have to go to their clan leader. Nobody wanted that. You didn't want to start trouble with other clans because you could bring a lot of misfortune.

People believed that if you fought over a particular spot, sometime later it would not bring in as much rice or pumpkins as you wanted it to. So you really didn't want to fight over it. If someone marked the spot, then other people had to respect that. It was a superstition.

❑

In Laos and now in America, if a clan leader calls for a clan meeting, all the men will go over to his house and talk about what it is they need to talk about.

Most of the time the women are not allowed to go to these meetings because the men feel that women talk too much. At the meeting, for example, if my father wanted to buy ten cows but didn't have enough money, he would go and ask the clan leader for help. The clan leader's job is to help, either by giving money or whatever. His job is to get all the clan members together and try to help him buy the ten cows. Then my father can buy the cows from another clan or people of a different nationality. As long as a member of the clan needs something, the rest of the members have a responsibility to come forward and help him.

Problems are always solved by the clan leader. For example, if my daughter were going to get married and my husband thought it was OK, but I didn't agree, we would take the issue to the clan leader and he would help us to decide.

❑

In Laos, my father was a missionary. He worked for a French Priest. His job was to go from village to village, teaching the Hmong how to live, and hopefully recruiting them into the Catholic Faith. Sometimes he would teach them a little Hmong, how to read and write. Other times he would preach about God.

My father learned to write in Hmong during the war, and then after the war he worked with a Priest. When he went from village to village, my mom and I had to go with him. It wasn't like a one-day trip. We would go for months.

Usually when we got to a village, they would already know we were coming, so there would be a little house waiting for us. And sometimes the people would feed us. The people were always receptive to us. They were warm to us.

☐

Most of the Hmong people believe in shamans, in life after death, and reincarnation. I am sure there is always going to be a conflict between Catholicism and the Hmong people.

It just depends on what you believe in.

PETER LEACH

Seng Yang

My dad's family had a huge farm with rice, corn, and vegetables. One person could not take care of it by himself. If my father was clearing his fields and had to chop down a big tree, he had to exchange labor. He got others to come chop the big tree down. They would bring their family to help him. Then my father would take his axe and help them chop down their trees.

They came and helped us, and then we went and helped them in exchange.

In just one or two days, the rice fields would be ready for planting; all the trees would be cut down. Having ten to twenty people working together made the work go faster. If we didn't work together, if it was just "one man, one man, one man," it would take months or years.

When it was harvest time, we would do the same thing. We would agree to finish my field first, then the neighbors, and so on. In this way it would only take a few days. If we worked alone it would take months. The more hands, the faster it went.

> We had to take our relationships with others into account when making decisions.

The head of the household, the husband and father, made decisions for the family. He had to work hard to find resources to support his family, and he also made the decisions. His wife and children were under his control. Our villages were small, and everyone knew each other very well. The man had to be sensitive to the family's relationships within the village.

There were also clan leaders in the village. If a family had a problem, they went to the clans to solve it. If the clan couldn't solve the problem, the leader would solve it—like a judge.

If a husband and a wife had a disagreement, they would go to the elders of the clan to discuss reconciliation of the problem. At the clan meetings, people sat in a circle around a fire. The husband and wife each had an opportunity to describe their problem to the circle, and the elders—both men and women—would listen and try to come to agreement about a solution.

For example, a couple once came to my clan to discuss their problems with the elders. They talked about the man's adultery. He was not taking care of his family, his children. He abused his wife. His wife was unhappy about this situation, so she brought it to the clan to solve.

If our clan could not solve it, she would bring it to her brothers and uncles. If that happened, we would have to pay money to their clan to fix the problem because the man, our cousin, was wrong. He was not a good household leader. He did not care for his family.

After the clan met with them, the husband agreed to stay with his wife and children and work harder to take care of them. If she needed something, he had the responsibility to provide it for her.

Through clan discussions like this, big problems became small and small problems disappeared.

> Life in Laos was tough for the Hmong people because of the war.

We moved from place to place, and we couldn't go back to our old villages from year to year. Every year, you had to prepare new rice and corn fields. We would lose land in one battle and win land in another, so our fields were constantly changing. We saw many disasters, but we had no choice. We had to protect our homeland, to keep the communist system out of our country. It was very difficult.

I left Laos in 1975. I crossed the Mekong River into Thailand soon after the peace agreement, which the communists soon violated, had been signed. I saw General Vang Pao, the leader of the Hmong, fly to

Thailand. I felt that with our leader gone, there was nothing we could do. So I took a taxi to the capital and hired a smuggling boat to carry me across the Mekong River to Thailand.

Because I left Laos very early, I didn't have to go through the jungle. The Hmong who came after 1976 had to come through the jungle.

Some people traveled to Thailand by car, some by boat, some by swimming. The rich and educated—those who could read about the situation, who knew that we were losing the war—came by boat and car. The people who didn't know, who thought we would still win, who wanted to fight until we won—these people had to walk through the jungle and escape by swimming or making boats from bamboo trees. They swam across the Mekong River. Many didn't make it. They were killed by the communists, or they drowned in the river.

In the refugee camps, we experienced more harsh times. There was no water or rice, and sanitation was very bad in the camps. A lot of people were sick; a lot of people died because of the lack of medicine, food, and first aid.

> I came to the United States in 1979. The first week after I arrived in Rhode Island, I rested. Then I got a job.

My sponsor found me a job making $3.00 an hour. I considered that good money! Later, I learned that if I spoke English I could get a better job. This was after four years of working on assembly lines, moving from job to job.

I didn't know how to get help from job services, how to get a better job. I couldn't drive. When it snowed, it was very cold waiting for the bus. I remember feeling like my ears were as hard as ice and being scared to touch them for fear that they would fall off.

We didn't know how to dress in the wintertime, with the cold weather and the wind chill. We didn't have heavy coats like the Americans. The weather was so different from our country. There were some Hmong who had come to the United States earlier, and they'd take us to a church to get a heavy coat and find heavy clothes. They'd help us get boots, instead of wearing sneakers.

> In 1984 I decided to resign from my job so I could get an education and learn more about this country and its culture. I needed to get a degree to make a better life for my family and myself.

I heard from my cousins and in-laws who lived here that there were opportunities to go to school in Minnesota. I moved to Minnesota in

1985. I went to adult education classes first, and then I went to community college. I finished community college in 1989.

I got a job in social services and attended Metro State University, where I was pursuing my BA degree. I worked full-time and went to school part-time. It was taking me too long, so I asked the agency to give me a leave of absence so that I could go to school full-time and finish faster. They agreed. I received my BA degree in 1996.

Now I'm working full-time, but I still take Continuing Education classes. I wish I had more brains and more energy so I could go another step. My bachelor's degree is just my first step, and I'd like to take the second step in this country. But I have a large family – 9 children and my wife. The children need support, so I have to work full-time.

Maybe five or ten years from now, when my children are grown up and can support themselves, I can go back to school.

> At home I speak Hmong and teach my children about our customs.

For example, I tell them they are from the Yang clan and they can't marry anyone with the same last name. They must know all my cousins and must call them by respectful names. For example, they should say "Uncle Khue", not Khue, not just his name. Saying only his name is not polite. They must call their brother-in-law's by their titles too. I teach them to respect their elders.

When they go to school I tell them to respect their teachers. If they have problems in school, they should ask questions of the teacher.

They are doing a good job of learning English in school all day and then speaking Hmong at home. If they go off alone, they speak English. If they come to me, they speak Hmong.

I want them to be bilingual so they will be more productive to this country. Once they are bilingual, they can be links. They can help connect the two cultures. They can tell people who don't speak Hmong what Hmong culture is about. Being bilingual is a skill they will be able to use through their whole lives. For example, at the University of Minnesota, they must know a second language, and I want to see that my children keep Hmong as their second language.

> There are conflicts between Hmong and American cultures.

Some children learn only from watching television, and their parents don't teach them differently. They see violence on TV, and then they join gangs. Their parents don't know how to handle this. Parents teach Hmong values and then schools often teach another way. Often, parents can't help their children with their homework because they can't speak the language. There is a lack of communication between parents and children.

If we had had a place like Jane Addams School twenty years ago—when we first came here—it would have helped our adjustment a lot. Jane Addams School is a place where the parents and the children can learn about Hmong history and the culture in the United States. Parents can then help their children succeed in this country.

I tell people that it's not too late. The parents who go to school at an old age are an example for their children. If we just stay home, our children will just want to stay home. My children ask me sometimes why I work all day and go to school. I tell them that if I didn't do this they would not have food or a good place to live. I tell them to work hard because our Hmong ancestors have always worked hard—from before the rooster crows until after the rooster goes to bed.

I would be ashamed to meet with our ancestors now because I have nothing—no farm, no land, no animals. I work for someone else and they give me what they can. I work to support my family. My children will have to work harder then I am now to have peace and rights. My children know that they have to study if they want to have a good life.

> I feel strongly that because of the nature of this country, the first generation of Hmong people will keep their culture, but the second generation will lose it.

The second generation will be busier, and they won't have as much chance to learn about it. There are Hmong living in Thailand, Laos, China, and France, and they still have a strong sense of the culture. In the United States, this is not true. Hmong-Americans have this sense of the culture in the first generation, but every generation that follows has less and less. Soon everyone will be mainstream.

The younger generation still needs to learn about Hmong culture, about things like the language and how to make Hmong clothing. It is difficult for them because they have to go to school and learn about other things. My children don't know how to sew because they don't have time. Education is a very important part of this country, so they have to become educated and can't take time to learn about their culture.

Jane Addams School can work to end this trend. A good example is See Moua, a student from the College of St. Catherine. When she first came to Jane Addams School, she didn't speak Hmong well, she didn't know Hmong culture well. Now she knows how to speak Hmong and knows more about Hmong culture. She can now help more Hmong people in the United States. The same thing happens for Hmong students from Humboldt High School who come to Jane Addams School. It even happens with some American students, like Jennifer. When she came back from Thailand she lost a lot of her Hmong, but Jane Addams School is helping her re-learn.

Jane Addams School teaches about Hmong culture. It shows that it's not a bad culture. It is good culture, a strong culture. We have to learn about American culture, and others have to learn about Hmong culture. They are equal. We share our culture with others, and they share their culture with us. Back and forth. You can see that the Hmong way of doing something is often different than the American way, but both are good.

> I am a Hmong-American. I feel that I work for my nation, the United States. I am working to build the nation.

The Hmong have been working for America for a long time. We worked with the American Central Intelligence Agency in Laos. Now that we are here, we continue to work for Americans. If I stayed on public assistance, I wouldn't contribute to the country. I must work and help my country

We have to work to be a part of this country, to make the country better. We have to work and keep alive so the country does not die. The country must get better, and the Hmong contribute to that.

> Our experience in Laos, not having freedom, was so different from what freedom means in the United States.

Because of this, many Hmong people don't know what freedom means here – like having the freedom to talk to the leadership of this country, having freedom to speak out and freedom to meet together. If a big group wants to get together, they can do it. When you say something here, you have freedom of speech, so you don't get in trouble. In Laos, if you said something against the government you got in trouble. Go against the government and you could get killed.

Freedom means if I want to do something, I can do it. If I don't know how to do something someone helps me do it. That's freedom to me. If I don't know something, someone teaches me. I'm free to learn about other cultures

In Laos, we didn't have the system we have here. Government was controlled by the "big guys," and you had to do as they said. You had to do whatever they wanted. The communists, those in power, controlled everything.

In Laos, we Hmong people didn't know freedom. We were always fighting and trying to protect ourselves. We were called "Meo"—like an animal—because we lived in the countryside. Hmong have more freedom in this country. We are not "Meo," we are Hmong; we are human beings who have freedom. The Hmong are starting to realize what this freedom means. We can travel the world legally. Go to France, Australia, China, America—wherever we want. We have permission to go.

At Jane Addams School, we are creating a democracy, creating freedom. The Hmong people say to me, "Wow we can talk now Seng. We can talk and have freedom of speech here and we didn't have that in Laos. We can talk to Senators and Representatives in this country."

We need naturalized citizenship for the Hmong elders. But the language requirement is a barrier for elder Hmong people. They cannot learn anymore. There should be freedom, too, for these people who cannot pass the test.

> The Hmong Unity Group, Hmoob Koom Siab, gets Hmong people together to learn about freedom and democracy in this country.

JOYCE YAMAMOTO

The Group is a combination of people from different clans. They can say anything they want in the meeting. If there is something they want to know, they can ask about it.

The Group has been working on welfare reform. Last year, we had good progress and got Senator Wellstone and Representative Vento to come to Neighborhood House to discuss the issue with us.

We told them about the struggles of the elders who are working to get their citizenship. Hmong people want to get their citizenship; then they will learn more English and go to work. Until then, we have no choice but to take assistance from the government. We only need help until we can get a job and be successful. The Hmong have no history of living on welfare.

We also told them about the Hmong veterans who had fought in the war in Laos. We talked about the construction of a monument for Hmong veterans who gave their lives for America. We talked about these issues with them.

> We have to work together. This is what democracy means to me.

The Humphrey Institute and Jane Addams School students have helped us by writing letters to their representatives and senators, urging them to co-sponsor the Hmong Veteran's bill. Jane Addams School works on political issues like this to put pressure on representatives to support Hmong issues. The first letter I got from Senator Grams did not look good, but now I see progress.

I think that in America, power can bring change. That power comes from the students and university professors, the staff at Neighborhood House, and the Hmong Unity Group all working together. It is power from the people.

At first, Vento's bill had no co-sponsors. Then he reintroduced it, and we pushed it through with the help of Jane Addams School and the college students. Now the bill has come back to life, and Senator Wellstone has introduced a similar bill in the Senate. This legislation is so important to the Hmong because it will help us to be self-sufficient.

The American government system puts the people in power. Power should be in the hands of the American people. In Laos, the Hmong were scared of the government. But they are not afraid of the American people. We can work together, Hmong and Americans. We have the power to change things.

> This is just the beginning for me.

After I left Laos I was angry. Our land was destroyed; now it is just a jungle. We have seen pictures of the places where our homes used to be. Now there is nothing. Our houses are gone; our old lives destroyed.

I was told that I could go to this new land, the United States, to resettle and have a new home. I took an oath that I would give up my homeland and go to a new country, a new nation.

I have worked to build my new home in this country. But this is just the first step. Now I have more work to do because there are still thousands of Hmong refugees who want to live with peace and freedom.

Nan Kari

I think my whole life has been about discovery. I have always loved to learn and often times, that learning has come through experiencing. Even as a child I can remember having ideas and seeing how those ideas were made concrete. And that's really what my works been about. It's what I write about. It's how I've thought of the work I did as an occupational therapist. The work at Jane Addams School is an idea being made concrete. That's kind of the frame I see my life in.

I grew up in the little town of Bemidji, which is in northern Minnesota. It's on a lake in the northwest woods near the headwaters of the Mississippi. I was outdoors all the time. There was a park right across the street from my house; lots of trees to hide out in, climb, places to have plays outdoors. So most of my growing up I was outdoors playing, doing tomboy-type stuff. But I also had really good friends who were girls. I never played with dolls. I was much more of an action person.

My family lived right across the street from a college, and I went to the laboratory school connected to the college. There was this fresh energy there, with lots of college kids teaching. They were excited about being teachers so I had a really positive experience at school. My life has always been attached, or attracted, to education in one way or another. I have taught at the College of St. Catherine for twenty-one years. I have always needed and loved schools and libraries.

I read a lot as a child. I read all the time, tons and tons of books; adventure books like Nancy Drew mysteries, and books about sailing. Then when I had kids of my own, that was one thing we did constantly. In fact, I read to my son Jonathon until he was in junior high. Then he wouldn't let me read anymore. I read both my children lots of philosophy stories, lots of stories about good and evil. It's another way of having adventures.

My dad owned a hardware store when I was a child. He was a really good man. It was in the working class part of town and there were lots of factories. Working class people would come shopping on payday. There was always this gathering at the store, and people would come and talk because my dad was a very congenial man. People came to his shop because he knew how to do everything. They would come in with this odd- looking thing and say, "Do you know how to replace this?" or "What do you do with this?" and he would know how to do all those things. It was a hardware store like the old fashioned ones—the ones that had bins of things and the shopkeeper was a craftsman. That is what my dad loved to do. Now when I go into that type of old hardware store— though there are not a lot around anymore—the smell takes me immediately back to the shop he had. The new ones don't smell the same.

My parents were hardworking people with lots of integrity. They were very community minded. They believed that if you worked hard your life would be a valuable life. Those values I carry with me. The work is different, but they influenced me a lot.

□

I got married when I was twenty-three years old. When you got married in those days, you didn't keep your maiden name. After a while I didn't feel I could change it back. By then, it seemed like I had grown into somebody that I associated with my new name. I came to understand myself to be Nan Kari. And it's a fine name. But if I were to marry now, I wouldn't change my name because it was like taking on a whole new identity that wasn't mine. It wasn't my history or who I was.

It took me a while to get my feet on the ground, figure out who I was. I didn't want to be a mother until I had some sense of that myself. Though at thirty-one, I certainly felt like an old mother. In those days, a lot of people were done having kids by that age.

My daughter is now fifteen and she is coming into her own, wondering what it means to be an Asian growing up in a family that is Caucasian. My son is twenty-one, trying to figure out what his life is and his work in the world. I have loved being a parent. I have always thought of it in terms of helping my children be who they are. They are very different from each other, which has forced me to be broader minded.

I think that good parents really help their children to ask the hardest questions: What is their life about, what is their work, who do they want to become, what do they want to accomplish? Reading those stories to them was a vehicle to do that. Stories were wonderful ways to talk about those questions. That is how I've seen my role as a mom—to talk about big ideas with little kids, to help them to see that they have as much to say about things, in their own way, as older people do.

One time I was in a rush, had to get to a meeting and was upstairs in my bedroom ironing something. I was late, I had to do a presentation. The phone rings and its Jonathon. He rarely calls me from college in Madison. I love it when he calls.

He said, "Mom..."

I cut him off, "Jon, I've gotta go..."

But he said, "I just have a quick question to ask you."

"OK, ask. I am ironing."

"Well, mom, what do you think about the existence of God...

I am doing this philosophy paper and I am supposed to critique the position of the author. But what do you think?"

I thought at the time how great that was. It reflects the kind of interaction that he and I have had over the years. That's what I've liked best about being a parent. I wouldn't have missed it for the world.

My husband and I had always thought that we would adopt a child, from the very beginning. I am sure I have been much more attentive to other cultures and traditions because we adopted a child from a different culture. It's part of my attraction to Jane Addams School. Learning about other cultures is really quite liberating because what seems to be fixed becomes much more fluid when you see that people do things other ways. It makes you reflect on your own traditions.

Because of Anna, I think of myself as partly connected to Korea. I like that—it gives me a reason to go there, to read about it, to have Korean things in my home. I like the idea of mixing cultures. For me, there was really no difference in adopting a child and birthing a child. Either it was my body that became the vehicle for bringing the child here or a plane. It didn't matter. The child belonged to me, a member of my family. That has been an important realization for me— that you can feel so strongly about people who do not come from your genetic background. I've felt it, I've learned it, I know it. I'm a better person for it.

□

When I was in college at the University of Wisconsin, the Vietnam War was in its heaviest years. Madison was a very beautiful campus. There were many hills and a lot of grass. It sits up on the side of a hill, and then down the hill is a walkway along the lake; so it is very beautiful. People were outdoors in Madison all the time. The streets ran through the campus. But during the war, the tensions around the college were so forceful, making Madison a hot bed. My last year at Madison, the National Guard was there the whole time, driving through campus in trucks with open backs, men with bayonets. The University felt so "occupied". I have vivid memories of the National Guard driving through those beautiful streets with fixed bayonets. The open trucks would let people out to guard all the doors. People with rifles guarded the doors to all the buildings.

Just yesterday when I was looking through my pictures, I came across a picture I had taken of the physics building that was blown out because the Army/Math Research Center was attached to the physics building. Two young men had put a bomb in the building. They had put it in at night, probably thinking that there wouldn't be anybody there. But there was a physics graduate student inside working. I remember his name. It was Robert Faschnat. He had two children. And he was killed. My roommate's boyfriend, who was also my friend, was a physics graduate student. He also spent full nights in the physics lab reading computer run-outs that would go all night. It could've been him. So I felt a real attachment to this person who died, though I never met him. It felt very real to me. I often wonder who he would've been, this man who died.

I should show you that picture of the building that was bombed. It's just a little photo but it has these explosive memories. I remember I was in bed when it happened. It was about four in the morning. I lived on campus, in an apartment right by and I heard the explosion. You know how explosions shake the windows and you hear this deep "BOOM"? Well, I knew something had happened but I didn't know what it was.

The Student Democratic Society had an active and strong chapter at Madison. Also strong were the beliefs that institutions were evil and that people had to step out of them; that the society that we were inheriting was wrong. There was a sense of thinking: students are powerful, students can shut things down, students can make a difference, students have an important voice. There were student rallies with hundreds of people. There was lots of rhetoric floating around in the air.

There was such a polarization between students and the police that things often became unnecessarily violent. There would be sit-ins and the police would come and throw tear gas, and everybody would panic. It was very scary. I remember one time when a riot began. I had a class in the business building; it was a very small building, only 3 floors. Dow Chemical had come to recruit. When I walked out of my class, the halls were filled with people and somebody was throwing tear gas. In the hall! I mean, it didn't make any sense. It was an emotional, bizarre situation. Whether or not people chose to be part of things, often times you just were.

It was also a very interesting time. The idea that students had a voice and that people were listening. We raised large questions of public morality, and the direction our country was going. That felt really good. But there was this other piece that made it very serious, and that was the loss of lives. People being beaten.

I remember walking down the street with my books in hand, just going home. There was this girl on her bicycle. She had long blond hair and a ponytail. She was a student, an ordinary person riding home on her bike. She had her books in the back. There were two policemen in front of me, and one of those policemen grabbed her by the hair and just yanked her off her bike. There was antagonism on both sides, but that kind of thing happened and made it very, very unsettling. Plus, it was all in the context of our country doing these incredible things, and people that I knew, people who were my age, who were on the other side of the world fighting in the war... it was a very odd time.

The war shaped my generation—whether you were a fighter in the war and came back to a country that was going to make you invisible or shame you for having done what you did or whether you fought against the war and believed that you could make change. It all has shaped our generation. I—and many others—have come away with this incredible belief that people can make a difference.

☐

Feelings about the war were never resolved for me because I graduated from Madison and just left. What else could I do? But it left unanswered questions in my mind:

> How do you make change? How do you influence social systems? How do you create democracy?

JOYCE YAMAMOTO

Those questions became enveloped in the work I pursued. One question I have thought about long and hard is this: How are movements for social change brought about? And how are they nurtured to create large stable transformation?

The Jane Addams School is an experiment in creating "a people's institution." Most importantly, it helps birth the movement happening now: People speaking up, telling the truth, who have a sense of urgency. I am involved with the Jane Addams School because of the people's potential there, and the social change that is being made. Most importantly, it helps me sort through unresolved questions I have about who I am, what social change is, and how to be effective in bringing that about.

We must work to create institutions that become vehicles for shaping the world. That is why joint ownership by everyone who comes there is so important; the idea that it can become a vehicle, influencing the neighborhood, state, the country. But how do you do that? How do you do that with people of such different cultures? At Jane Addams School we get to learn how to do that, and in a way that draws on the talents of many different kinds of people. It is so important for us to know this, in terms of what we have to do in our country.

Jane Addams will always be influenced by the people who are there. We must make sure not to be so rigid and tight; to allow that fluidity, so that it doesn't lose its purpose or value but it is indeed shaped by the needs and desires of the people who are part of it. As other people come, it will perhaps take on a different form. But that is the fun of it. And that is what institutions need to learn how to do—how to refresh themselves; that's what we don't do so well in institutional lives today.

I remember one time, Nan Skelton was so inspiring to me—this was before we created Jane Addams School—"Institutions need a way that they can refresh themselves. They need to be attached to things that are part of them but are also outside of them." She said it in a much more eloquent way, but that was sort of the inspiration of Jane Addams School. That it would be attached to the NH, College of St. Kates and the University but at the same time not be. So we could go back to our institutions with this "Jane Addams" experience and influence the practices there. Influence the teaching practices, scholarship practices, professional practices of the people who work there and the people "using those services". Start to change the dynamics.

□

What are the elements for community learning that would lead to a deeper understanding of citizenship? This is the question that Nan Skelton and I studied for a year after getting some grant money to work on civic education. We wanted to create a link between a community organization and college students and develop a model of learning based on reciprocity. We tried to figure out how and where to create a community-based "school". Talking to Sandy Fuller, Program Director of Neighborhood House, we realized she was more than ready for this type of challenge. And with the addition of John Wallace, University of Minnesota Philosophy professor, we met from April to August, deciding in the end to just do it!

The Hmong people showed up in droves for the first scheduled meeting where we discussed the idea of the school with residents of the West Side. It took all our juices to try to manage. With no curriculum, it was not your typical "school," but the Hmong people wanted to focus on citizenship, so they used the 100 questions and practiced English while also getting to know everyone and teach about Hmong culture.

My vision for Jane Addams School is that it is a modern day Hull House. A people's democratic institution claimed by the people, where the colleges act as resources for different kinds of learning. People connect their everyday lives to it. Own it. What you can do, you do with other people. It should be a power base that can influence public policy. I see the Jane Addams School as a creation for the democratic movement, a vehicle for that movement. I believe institutions are going to be key in making fundamental changes in society. We learned this from the Civil Rights and Anti-War Movements. The Jane Addams School will not achieve these goals if it is seen as a program only to help people. It must be a visible community-based program that works for increased freedom.

Freedom is the collective ability to shape our lives together, to create a common destiny, so we don't do it as a detached people, but as A people. It is a struggle to be free because you have to liberate yourself from the rules handed down to you, and the way you were reared. It is a task for all of us to listen to the ways in which we are called forth, to liberate our spirits, to trust that freedom is necessary. There are a lot of constraints in doing this. To obtain freedom is a radical act. It is about individual and collective identity. We need to spend time looking back into our basic assumptions and either claim or reshape them. What do those sacred values mean? Freedom! The ability and courage to do just that!

PETER LEACH

The key is to see democracy as an unfinished task.

This calls for everyone's contributions, newly arrived immigrants included. In America many have lost oral traditions, but some new immigrant groups have not. What can we learn from them?

Stories shape America.

We are learning from other people's stories and our own.

"The Jane Addams School gives me more opportunity to bridge understandings and cultures."

See Moua

Section 6
See Moua

Aleida Benitez

"A Boy Named Joe"

"Loving People First"

See Moua

I was born in a refugee camp in Nong Khai, Thailand. It was 1975, when the Vietnam War had just ended. I was the seventh of eight children. Families were starting to go to the United States, but we lived in Thailand for three and a half more years. During that time, I was unable to speak. My mother called it "frozen tongue". I had a lot of health problems, and we had no money to take care of them.

Before my parents came to Thailand, they escaped from Laos by hiding in the jungles. It was a safer time but soldiers were still patrolling that area. My dad worked for a CIA sponsored group under the leadership of General Vang Pao. He oversaw pilots. That is how he learned to speak Thai. There were Thai fishermen in the Mekong River and because my dad was able to speak to them in Thai, he helped some of them when their boat got stuck. In turn, they helped my family escape from Laos. At that time, my mother was pregnant with me.

I was born in Thailand a few months after my family arrived. While traveling, my mother had four children under the age of ten. Two children had passed away before they were able to make the trip. As soon as the rest of the family got to Thailand, they were all taken to the refugee camp. My parents don't talk much about it. I don't have any images of the neighborhood or houses or anything. But they tell me of this pond where they used to threaten to throw me in—because I was such a difficult baby.

> I have visions of this pond. My mom says they have cleared it now to build houses.

I muttered some sounds my first four years, but nothing much. I was really small, and that is how I got my Hmong nickname "Me," which means "small." My parents still call me that, even today. My new United States citizen name is See Elissa Moua. My sister and I used to watch "Married with Children," and she would say that I reminded her of Al Bundy because I walk with my shoulders down, drooping. So she started calling me "Al", and that is where Elissa came from. I've started using this name on forms. I decided to add this name because now that I am a citizen, I wanted an American name. I am still very proud of my Hmong name, but it felt very official to have this change. My brother says, "Elissa will be like a new person," which is good and bad. But I could never drop my name See. I like it. It's simple.

My mom and dad got a divorce right before coming to America. They had personal problems, and my dad found out he couldn't have more that one wife in America. My mom was his first wife, but he also had a second wife. Even though they were going to get a divorce anyway, he was angry with the law. Maybe he misunderstood the law and was afraid he couldn't be a part of his children's lives anymore, so he felt guilty and didn't want his kids to hate him. My dad got a divorce from his second wife too because of marital problems. These two divorces in a short amount of time were very uncommon.

My dad had a lot of authority, power and wealth. He got married to his present wife, who was very young, soon after the divorces went through. My dad is a very strong Hmong man and he wanted to save face. His divorces kind of devastated him. My mom is very respectful of him and careful not to make him look bad.

My family came to the United States together, so my dad stayed with us at our cousin's house in Minnesota for a couple years before we were able to move out; before my dad got a job. It was when we moved out that his wife came to live with us. That was tough, but she was very young and didn't have any children yet, so she took care of me. My dad didn't want to just leave us, so we lived like that for a year or two. My mom couldn't work because of us kids. He helped her get on welfare before he left us. I didn't know my parents were divorced until much later, and I didn't realize who his wife was. When I was seven years old, his wife had her own kids and she didn't take care of me or come around anymore. That is when I started to realize my dad had his own family.

When we got the United States in 1980, I was four and a half years old and speaking came really fast all of a sudden. I spoke both English and Hmong, because I was put into preschool right away. I was still a shy kid even in kindergarten, so translators would call my mom and ask if I had mental problems, saying I wouldn't play with anyone. Then they called about putting me in an ESL program, which they did. After that, they stopped calling, except to ask my mom why she hadn't signed permission slips. In second grade, more Hmong started coming to the United States and to school, so it helped me build confidence and was good for my English and Hmong language learning too. I had two really good Hmong friends and we would always hang out. The teacher would separate us because she wanted us to meet other kids.

There were lots of Hmong in junior high school. This was the first time in my life I didn't like being Hmong. There was this little gang, mostly made up of Hmong, that caused a lot of trouble and police often had to come to school and I hated that. I didn't like identifying myself with the Hmong at all. I would separate myself from Hmong events in school and the community. I did have Hmong friends, but they felt the same way I did.

But my junior high school social studies teacher, Mr. Theune, had a special interest in Hmong culture. He would have us talk about our culture and bring things to show. He would show movies about other cultures with other people of color who I could look up to. He taught me to be proud of my own culture, my own people. So I left junior high school feeling torn from the way I used to think, with a new perspective because of my teacher.

At Johnson High School there was a large population of Hmong. I joined the Asian club and it helped me not feel so different. Senior year I was president of it. The idea of getting away from Hmong people, and even my family, started to come back around the time I was getting out of high school. My mom was still on welfare, which hadn't bothered me before, but it really motivated me to do something about my own situation. I felt bad for my mom, but I couldn't do anything for her. So I wanted to get away, separate myself from it. She didn't want me to go.

> "What would Hmong people think of you? You are a Hmong woman. What will they think of you going away? Maybe they will think you are not Hmong enough, going away and living on your own. And I will miss you."

So I decided to stay. I went to St. Kate's, which was my second choice anyway. But I had to convince my mom to let me stay in the dorms because she was still worried about what people would think. After the first year she trusted me more, but I got busy my later years in college, and couldn't call or come home as much.

> "What is college doing to you?" she would ask.

She and I had a crying session because she wanted me to come home more, to learn how to cook and clean like a good Hmong girl. But I told her I wouldn't.

I still feel guilty about it. She still cooks and cleans for me. She shouldn't have to but she wants to and doesn't want me to take time away from my studies. I guess I had it easy. I feel very fortunate. Other Hmong girls my age had responsibilities of cooking and cleaning, but I

JOYCE YAMAMOTO

didn't. Many of my childhood friends are married and have moved away. They were pressured to quit school and to take on those other responsibilities.

But when we were young we all talked about our dreams—dreams of school, professions…

Even though I didn't have my dad around growing up, I was able to do many things. College scholarships were granted to me mostly because my father was not around. If he would have had to work to pay for my school, I don't know how things would have been.

I still see him once in a while. Just last week, I went out with him. It was the first time that I had ever gone out with him in a small group. My sister went too. He looked really tired and disturbed. I asked him what was wrong,

> "Tell us what you are feeling."

He wouldn't, but I could see his frustration turn to sadness, and then finally he talked. He was feeling guilty. He hadn't had much to do with our lives and then here we were taking him out to eat.

After the meal, he gave us both hugs, which is something uncommon for older generation Hmong parents because they don't like to express a lot of their emotions, physically or verbally. That really bothers me because I never really understand if they care. When my parents did show emotion, it was the opposite of that they meant. For example, my mom would always say, "stay home, relax about school" when really she wanted me to succeed in school.

I think I surprised my dad a lot. He always had hopes for his sons and the things they would do. Not that he didn't care for me, he just didn't put his energies in me as much. So when he found out all I did, he was shocked. But I don't do things to get back at him. I don't say, "Yeah, I am a girl and I did all that!"

I am doing it for myself. If it opens his eyes that's great, but it shouldn't be the reason I am doing what I am doing. I used to be mad at him for not being around, and felt as though I did everything all on my own. But now I feel as though I want to help him, along with my mom. I encourage him to take time out for his children. My mom was so busy taking care of all of us that she couldn't spend individual time with us. So I encourage my dad to do it now. He works up to twelve hours a day though.

The best thing my parents taught me is to respect who I am, to be humble, and respect other people. I learned the last one indirectly from them because they felt elders always knew more. My father believes males are always right. I learned from the way he is.

The Jane Addams School gives me more opportunity to bridge understandings and cultures. I definitely want Hmong culture to be a part of my life, as well as my children's when I have them. Learning the Hmong language is important.

My mom used to say,

> "You can go far by going to school or getting a good job, but if you can't come back and help the Hmong people, you haven't done anything. If you can't speak Hmong and don't know the culture, how will you help people?"

With this in mind, I want this for my children—a sense of responsibility to Hmong people and the larger surrounding community. It is important to remember we, the Hmong, aren't in the United States because of ourselves. Many people helped us along the way. We must help other people too. Community is a big cycle of helping people. I want my children to know this!

JOYCE YAMAMOTO

Journal Entries: Reflections on the Building of Relationships
October 1, 1999

Today is my first actual day as a Jane Addams School intern, so to speak. And today will be my first day with the kids too. I am excited. I haven't been able to see them much at all when I have been working with the adults. It's almost like they are in their own little world. And I am in my own little world. It would be good to see the groups together more often, to have activities that would bring them together. Think about all the chaos we will have though! But then again, think of all the interesting things we can learn from this as well as from each other. Both the children and adults have so much talent and so much to give; the only problem is that they don't have avenues to use them. Some don't even realize what it is they do have. Through my position, and as a bridge between the adults and children, I hope I can help to make this happen.

November 5, 1999

The children's activity went great tonight. We made necklaces. I was a little hesitant about everyone, including the boys, making necklaces but they all actually liked the activity. The boys especially. At first, some of them seemed disgusted with the idea, but once they got going, the liked it a lot. Some of the older boys even made two or three necklaces.

Gosh, the kids amaze me. They have so much energy, so much creativity. It just shows in the things they make. One of the boys was about to design a pattern in his necklace, so that it wasn't just a haphazard stringing together of beads and pasta pieces. He even carefully picked the colors and combination. It was fall colors, natural tones of brown, brick reds, yellow, and oranges.

November 10, 1999

It dawned on me today when I saw Mr. Her, one of the parents in the adult learning circle, that I forgot to mention in my last entry about how he came into the children's circle and told ghost stories during the week of Halloween. The kids just loved it when he came. He told the scary stories in Hmong and I translated them into English. It was good to have him come and tell the stories—some time for the children and parents, particularly Mr. Her, to be together. Mr. Her's own kids were there and it was especially good to see how one of his kids told everyone to be quiet and listen because "my dad is talking". The little boy is identifying with and is proud of his dad. He is respectful of his dad and wants others to be as well.

December 8, 1999

Today the adults in the Hmong circle threw a big surprise party for all the students and "teachers" as they call us, even though we are all teachers and learners here. The kids all went to it and got some food to eat. They got a chance to socialize with their friends and parents. Mainly Hmong food was brought, so they were able to teach the college students about the different food, their contents, and even possibly how their parents might have made it. It was interesting to hear one little boy's story about how his mother made the rice. He said something like; "You can't eat the rice until it is cooked, because it is still hard. You're going to break your teeth if you try. My mommy put the rice in a pit and let it sit there for a long time until the rice got soft."

Food is definitely a good opportunity to teach others… there was a dish made up of tapioca and coconut juice that many people seemed to like. The woman who made it just stood there for nearly five minutes explaining it to everyone who was interested.

The Hmong often think they don't have anything to teach. But when you have something such as food that is physical and real, it is much easier for the Hmong elders, and people in general, to talk about it, relate to it, and teach about it. When you have abstract concepts such as democracy, the constitution, and freedom, it is harder. Because of all the time spent in a war-stricken country, running for their lives, the Hmong actually do know a lot about freedom and what it really means to be free. Some of them just haven't made the connection between that and what they are learning right now. The problem is how to make it so that they can relate their own experiences to what they are currently trying to learn.

December 15, 1997

Tonight's the last night we are meeting before going on break. We are breaking until January 5th. I will surely miss seeing the children for the next few weeks. I have just begun to really connect and bond with some of them. One little girl calls me "older sister" and always asks for me when I am not there. The boys and I are finally starting to talk on the same level. I have never written about this before, but it has been really hard for me and the rest of the other female college students to be able to connect with them. I am just starting to understand how to work with these boys a little bit better, but now I won't get to see them for the next month. It will be kind of sad. I will miss them.

Aleida Benitez

My family and I moved to the United States from El Salvador when I was about six years old. We left my grandmother, who had taken care of us for three or four years in El Salvador, and went with our mother. That was the most powerful experience I had at that age. It was really difficult to get used to being in the United States, having to learn English, and leaving my grandmother behind. That was one of the things I remember most.

Playing with all the other little kids in El Salvador was a lot of fun. We had tons of little friends. But then we also knew that there was a civil war going on and that the older kids were being pulled into the army. When we were living there, we were always afraid of airplanes. Whenever they went by, we would look up and wonder what was going on, where they were going to bomb next. We made our life seem as natural as possible, but in the back of our heads we knew something else was going on. We went on with our everyday routines, but we knew that our country was at war. Our main transportation was the bus, and every time we went to the city or market, there would be searches on the way there. We made it part of our routine to be stopped and stared at by the military.

My mom left El Salvador for a number of reasons. It was the early eighties. She didn't have a job, was in the middle of a really bad divorce, and a civil war was going on. She didn't have anywhere else to go, so she just wanted to get out really fast and escape to the United States. She promised she would come back for us kids later when she had a good job and a good home. She left my sisters and me with our grandma for three years.

My grandma made it as comfortable and natural as it could possibly be living without our mother. She was the most nurturing person. She loved us to death, and always reminded us that our mother would come back. She made it seem like the most natural thing to happen: that your mother would leave for three years or so and then she would come back.

Grandma never really punished us. For some reason she thought that us listening to her stories was a punishment. She would tell us fairytales, stories with good moral ideas. Don't lie—even though things are not going your way now, if you are honest, things will eventually turn out good. She constantly told us these stories. She told us the story of Cinderella, but she told it in a way that made it feel like town gossip.

> "There was this poor girl, she was doing everything right, but nothing was going her way. All of a sudden a prince shows up and carries her away. Her stepsisters are so jealous of her, but they didn't deserve him. They weren't doing everything right in their lives."
> "Grandma, how do you know the story?"
> "Well, you see, I was the cook in the kitchen. You should've seen the wedding dress she was wearing. Oh, and that wedding cake... the most beautiful cake I ever saw...it had three or four tiers."

We began to think that if she was there, she must know.

Every week, she would tell us stories like that; about girls who, even though they needed something, didn't steal because it wasn't right. I think those stories helped me to figure out what was right and what was not, without being punished for it.

But one time she got really angry! My older sister and I would get water from the well, and she made ceramic jars for us to carry back the water, but we would always break them. We were supposed to carry them on our heads, and we would be walking and shaking our hips too much or chasing boys and falling down. She was really tired of us always falling and breaking the jars, so she told us we would have to be punished for it.

> "Oh grandma, you never punish us."
> She got this jug of corn and she threw it on the ground.
> "O.K. pick it up! Go on your hands and knees and pick up every little piece of corn."

There must have been a hundred or so pieces.

She was mad because we were laughing, but we couldn't stop. It was just so unnatural for her to be punishing us. I remember it was a punishment but that it also was really fun. I know why she did it, and I thought that maybe we should be more careful, but it wasn't an awful punishment at all. That was the way she did it. She was really kind, not cruel, and made it fun to be punished.

My mom and my grandmother made a decision not to have us kids see any of the war, if at all possible. Anytime we walked into a room when people were talking about it, they would shut up. Anytime the radio would begin to report on the war, they would shut it off. Every time we went to the market by bus and there was gunfire, they would make us drop down on the seats. So in a lot of ways, I lived in this innocent world.

The funny thing is that since coming to the United States, people make me feel like I have to justify the war—a war I don't remember at all because my mom and grandma kept it from me. So either I would seem pretty ignorant or I would have to teach myself what happened during the war.

I remember the war from the perspective of a six-year-old. But I've read books, and I've taught myself what happened. It seems weird to read about something I was in, but didn't know much about. I start to wonder whether or not I should've known more about it. But I didn't have much choice. When I was older, I did a lot of talking to my grandmother and mother about it.

"Did anyone you know die? What happened? How did the war affect you? What were you doing when this was going on?"

And they know that I am getting a lot of that from facts I've read. I think they understand now that I want to know a little more than just the basic idea that there was a war going on around me back in El Salvador.

When we came to the United States and I started going to public schools, it was really hard for me because I didn't speak English. All of a sudden we were put into these places where we had to speak English. We lived in Houston, Texas, and there were no ESL classes. But I got really lucky. I had a teacher who knew that I was completely terrified of my situation, so she made me as much a part of the class as possible. But she also knew I was not keeping up or learning any English, so she would keep me after school, and we would read together. Then she would give me a ride, and she would either take me to the ice cream parlor or to get a piece of candy. Then I would go home. I thought that was the coolest thing in the world. My mom probably thought it was normal, a lot of the teachers in El Salvador do that too. But that teacher was extremely unique. Most teachers here don't do that.

But in second grade, I had a really bad experience with a teacher who did not like me at all. She was the opposite of my first grade teacher. She didn't want me to be a part of her classroom at all. She wanted me as far away from her and the other students as possible. She would tell me that I interrupted her English. The funny thing about her was that she knew Spanish, but she tried to make it seem like she didn't. She would never translate what people said for me. Her method of dealing with me was to put my desk against the wall and make me read to myself for two or three hours, just staring at the wall. She wouldn't let me go to recess. She later told my mother that I wasn't smart enough to go on to third grade, so she failed me.

She made it known to me that I wasn't as smart as everybody else was. I was just a burden to her.

I stopped struggling with English when I was in 6th grade. I had a bunch of special reading classes, in 4th and 5th grade especially, that I was taken out of regular class for. Around that time, my older sister told me, "When you stop dreaming in Spanish, that is when you know English well." And in 6th grade, I stopped dreaming in Spanish. I remember it because I was waiting for the moment when I would know English well. Another example is when you stop counting in Spanish in your head, when you are doing your math and you think "two plus two" instead of "dos y dos".

That doesn't necessarily mean my life was better after I knew English, but it was a lot easier for me to get to know other kids.

Because of all the struggles we had gone through, my mom made a conscious decision to keep us in very "white" schools so it would be easier for us to learn the way to interact with people. To me, it seemed normal because I knew I was in the US and would be with American kids. But looking back, there were lots of Mexican kids going through the same things we were. Only we were in isolation. Probably starting in 3rd or 4th grade all the way up, we were in schools that were as "white" as possible.

We stayed in Texas for six years. From there we moved to Appleton, Wisconsin. We stayed there for seven years. We moved around a lot because my mom was looking for the right place. San Antonio was OK, but she was looking for somewhere quieter. We stayed on a ranch that was nice because my mom could do her own farming and plant her own vegetables. She liked working there and she liked growing her own food. But we left for Wisconsin because a friend had told her there were really good jobs and schools there. It worked out well for her.

One thing that has really affected who I am is that I have had super strong women around me. My mom is one. She did not want to come to the U.S. If there had been other choices, she wouldn't have left El Salvador. She had to, and so she made it work for her. My grandma is one of the strongest ladies I know, too. Her husband died when my mom was really young. But grandma didn't let anybody tell her that she couldn't do something, that "she was only a woman." She did the best she could and raised her daughters the best she knew how. She made them go as far as they could in their education. She gave them good moral values. It's weird, but I have always been surrounded by only women.

Going to college has made me realize that there are such things as traditions. I read about "what immigrant people do." But when I was growing up they were not traditions. They were everyday things, everyday values that were just a part of my life. So I guess I do have a lot of traditions. One is that I speak Spanish. Others are the family values that I have. It is amazing to me how my friends see their family as "way out there" because with my mom and my sisters, we always help each other out.

If my car breaks down and I don't have money, my younger sister will give me one hundred dollars, my older sister will give me two hundred, and my mom will pay the rest. That is the way we figure things out. I know that is probably due to the fact that we came to this country and we had no one else, so we had to support each other. But that is also a traditionally Hispanic value. We have female cousins who we call "aunts" and male cousins we call "uncles". We have an extended family that is always looking out for us. They ask, "What are you doing in school? How are you doing? What's going on with your life?"

The type of food we eat is another tradition being passed down without my even being aware of it. To me, it's just memorizing how to cook lots of good food.

Eventually, I'd like to figure out how I identify myself within the larger American culture. But for me, that is an ongoing question. I don't want to close myself off as "Hispanic-American" or just "American". I don't want that to form who I become. I want to form it. For some reason, what is out there doesn't seem to fit me. I don't want to fall into a category because it closes off a lot of opportunities for me to be who I can become.

I come from a world of Spanish, and I want my children to know that. Maybe they will even learn Spanish and know who I was. Knowing that my children will probably be a little bit more integrated or assimilated than I was, it will be important for them to know our history without having to read it in some book. They will have the choice to accept it, to learn more about it, or just to keep it for future reference.

At different times in my life, freedom has meant different things. Before I came to the United States, freedom meant the obvious: getting out of a country that could no longer be yours because it couldn't shelter you or give you food. You just couldn't live there anymore. So you had to get out of this poverty-stricken country. That was freedom.

Now, freedom is accumulating and gathering up all these things I was and am becoming, being aware of them and merging them into one. Being completely free to be myself. Freedom to be comfortable with who I am.

To me, it means being comfortable being bilingual and Salvadoran, but knowing I probably have a better understanding of America than anything else. It means recognizing that different things have shaped who I am. But that is a lifetime goal. I do not plan on accomplishing all that tomorrow. Probably when I am sixty-five.

I remember when John Wallace told me about Jane Addams School and how I could work with the Hispanic community of the West Side of St. Paul. I thought that would be really good for me because I don't practice my Spanish enough and I don't hang around people that are "Latinos" very much. I went in thinking that I could give something back, that I could give Spanish and English back.

Only, I was drawn into another struggle—a common struggle of being an immigrant child. I started feeling that with the Hmong children. What it means to be growing up with another language that is seemingly obscure and clumsy because it doesn't fit in the English world. Seeing that in the kids at Jane Addams School, I really understood it, and I wanted to hang out with them.

I saw a lot of myself in those kids. For some reason, I felt that the children and I communicated quite well. It probably was a combination of who I was and what went on in my life at the time I was their age. The kids knew that I wanted to communicate with them, though I didn't speak their language. We shared a basic language of "hello" and "hi." You can communicate really well with a four-year-old even though you don't speak or act like them, even if you aren't Hmong.

When I started college, my mom basically told me to get a degree, get out and get a job. And that's what I was going for. It felt so weird because it didn't seem to fit me, but I had to go for it because it was the only option I was given. Going to Jane Addams School, I started realizing that you can create your job. Not only that, but what your job is can help shape who you are. Your job and the work you do can be those passions you feel inside.

That person you're striving to be. It can all become one.

I thought that that was a privilege; for someone who already has a lot of money. But I am starting to see that it is just about how badly you want it. How badly you want that to become you. My work at Jane Addams School has made me realize that I want it pretty badly.

That realization started me thinking that my mom worked really hard to get us to where we are. She worked at every job you can imagine. She worked three or four jobs a week to put food on the table, to pay rent, to pay for the car, everything. She worked with her body. She put everything into it, her muscles, everything. So I thought that was the person I would have to become. But I know she wasn't really happy. She would get home and be crabby. Sometimes she'd take it out on us, but that was who she was. And I started realizing that this wasn't who I had to become. I like knowing this, but it also makes me feel bad. I start thinking who my mom could've become if things had been different.

Working in the Children's Circle also helped me realize that I'd forgotten what it was like to be a child. I love seeing how kids make sense of their world. They don't have any boundaries or any adult close-minded views. They can be as creative or abstract as anything in the world; but that is the way they see things and that is what you have to go by. I love how kids challenge me every day to see things differently.

JOYCE YAMAMOTO

At Jane Addams School, the work is genuine. Everything you do is human nature, because it's your passion, it's the kind of person you are. Generosity and love are communicated to other people. You're there with friends.

I like feeling all that passion as soon as I walk in. Everyone comes from completely different roads, with different mindsets. But they are there because of passion for what they are doing. We may have different perspectives and may be getting different things out of our experiences at Jane Addams School, but we're all in it because of that person we are striving to become! The residents, the kids, the university students—we are all at Jane Addams School with many, many passions. But we work together, so in a way, they are all the same passions.

I am being created by what Jane Addams School offers. I don't see myself as a creator as much as I am being created by all the elements there—the energy, the need—they drive me. Jane Addams School creates me.

It's changed me a lot in the past two years. To some extent I have hated it because I've really had to dig up all these skeletons I hate about myself. But what drives me to this place, to come every Monday and Wednesday and to all the meetings is that I realize it is just so much a part of me that I start doing more and more. I start reading about it, taking classes on it, and going to extra meetings. In many ways I never saw myself liking it as much as I do. But once this work drags you in, it really drags you in. It gets you because it makes you question any and everything you've learned. It makes you question who you've become. And it makes you realize how much you don't know. So you always have to reinvent yourself at the start of a night. I like all those aspects of it. They contradict each other.

PETER LEACH

"A Boy Named Joe"

By Aleida Benitez

Over the past two years, I have built a friendship with a seven-year-old boy named Joseph. Today in a room full of twenty-some other young people, Joe came up to me and grabbed my hand. With his other hand he pointed in the direction of a kid who looked to be about twelve years old.

> "Aleida!" Joe said.
> "You need to kick that kid out of here. Kids who wear baggy pants are robbers!"

When Joe told me this, I didn't stop to think of how silly his comment sounded. I only knew that his voice sounded very sincere. Joe and I started walking towards the person he was accusing.

"Him!" he said. "He is wearing baggy pants so he is a robber!"

At this point Joe and I are still holding hands. I ask the boy who is wearing the baggy pants if he could talk to us for a bit. The kid looked up wondering if he had done something wrong. I assured him there was nothing wrong, but could he talk to Joe and me for a couple minutes? We walked towards the hallway and sat on a couch. I explained Joe's logic to him. I also told him to try to take this issue with all seriousness because to Joe, who was sitting as far away as possible from us on the couch, it was very serious. I explained that Joe believes all kids who wear baggy pants are robbers or bad people. Joe jumped into the conversation by adding that his sister has a boyfriend who wears baggy pants, and he is a robber.

"Well," the kid said. "I am not a bad kid."

But Joe didn't seem satisfied with this answer.

"Yeah, but you are wearing baggy pants!"

We sat with Joe for a couple minutes explaining to him that not all kids who wear baggy pants are bad. As we talked, Joe moved closer and closer to us. But by the end of the conversation, he was still not convinced that the kid he had pointed to was not a robber. He couldn't understand why his logic had failed.

Joe's experience makes me realize how lucky I am to be working in an environment where children allow me to see and understand how they make sense of their world. With time Joe's ideas will change. Soon he will no longer be afraid of kids who wear baggy pants.

But for now this is the way he makes sense of the world.

JOYCE YAMAMOTO

"Loving People First"

By Gunnar Liden

The idea of education as a process of loving and respecting all people everywhere, including children, became a reality through my experience at the Jane Addams School for Democracy. In changing my field of study from psychology to philosophy, I added many education and social justice courses which helped shape my understanding of what good education is. But I was still stuck in an impersonal, non-liberating concept of education. I expressed my discontent with the current state of education to John Wallace, my philosophy professor. He told me about some "amazing work" being done at the Jane Addams School, which might be "what you are looking for."

I walked into Neighborhood House on the West Side of St. Paul, not knowing anything about Jane Addams School or who the Hmong were, nor did I have any prior English as a Second Language (ESL) training. Very quickly I learned that I did not need it. Shortly after sitting down at a table with five Hmong women and two other college students, someone announced that we should start the "cultural exchange." The night's topic was "the treatment of elders within society."

After the facilitator announced this in English, Chong, a bilingual woman, translated it into Hmong. I was surprised that right after the translation, there was immediate commotion and conversation among the Hmong residents. Chong quickly translated.

"Why do we put our parents in nursing homes?

Why would we do this if we love and respect them?"

There was no room for superficial academic discourse about the way things should be or how we would like to think they are. The people wanted straightforward responses. There was a long silence, for none of the college students had an answer. I felt this sense of guilt. While there are many reasons for the existence of nursing homes—economics, individuality, time—all of these seemed like excuses and rationalizations rather than true answers.

The Hmong adults moved into the silence and explained why respect for their elders is a necessity no matter what society they are in. I recognized the beauty of what they were saying. Respect for life should have no societal boundaries. In a brief half hour, I had not taught one thing, but rather learned something of great value from those who I thought I was supposed to be teaching. I experienced that education can be a reciprocal activity in which everybody is a teacher and everybody is a learner, and for the first time I felt liberated by this idea that education is a living thing.

My next challenge was to find a way to make the work on the citizenship exam real. Working out of the green citizenship folder is safe and relatively easy to do.

> "What are the colors of our flag? What is the supreme law of the land? Who elects the president?"

There is nothing in these questions or this process that relates to being human or to being a citizen. I felt disrespectful telling the Hmong students how they should respond by giving a pat answer.

About a month into my work at Jane Addams, the citizenship work began to come alive. As I sat next to my learning partner Zoua, it was obvious to both of us that we were getting bored going over the same questions again and again. As we switched to writing some of the practice sentences, Zoua exclaimed, "You say too!" I repeated the sentence that she had just copied down, "My name is Gunnar." As I pointed to the next sentence for her to copy she said, "No. Say Hmong. Kuv lub npe hu ua Gunnar."

As I struggled just to be able to pronounce it in a way that was acceptable to her, I could not help but grin ear to ear as I felt life come back into our learning. For the last hour of that night, we worked as a team, neither of us more of an expert than the other (even though her English far surpassed my Hmong). Not only did I feel as though this reciprocal learning was full of life, but the learning stopped being about the citizenship test and started to be about us as teachers for each other. We were helping each other understand the "other's" world.

Success happened. First, we were both forced to understand what the other was saying. It is often hard to come to terms with the fact that the person you are working with, even if they know the right answer to the question, has no clue what it is they or you are saying. As Zoua and I continued, these English words that we were constantly writing and speaking, finally had life. Similarly, Hmong was not some faraway language for me now, but it became a medium for our discussion. To be able to teach me the Hmong, she had to understand the English, and vice versa. More importantly though, we were able to start a relationship beyond the citizenship exam, beyond teacher and learner, and beyond college student and Hmong resident.

When we worked on the sentence about where she worked, we both shared what work was like for us. When she wrote down how many children she had, along with teaching me the Hmong translation, she told me their names, brought out pictures of them and talked about the loss of her family when she left Laos. I, in turn, talked and shared pictures of my family, showed her how far Pittsburgh (my hometown) is from St. Paul, answered and discussed her questions about why I live so far from my family and why I did not have any children. We were relating to each other as human beings. I had no idea whether I was the teacher or the learner, and I finally knew that I had experienced the type of education I was longing for.

In the "adult circle" one night, when it came time to get with a learning partner, there was no one for me. Looking at this as an opportunity rather than a dilemma, I ventured into the Youth Center to work with the "children's circle" for the night. I had seen most of these kids before, because I was working with their parents in the "adult circle." However, I really did not know any of them. As I opened the door, "chaos" was the only word that came to my mind. Fifty kids were doing fifty different things, most of them speaking a language I could not understand. I felt insecure about how to relate to these kids. But not for long because being one of two male volunteers in the room, my role was designated to me by the kids very quickly...human jungle gym. At the end of the night, as Meng, Joe, Sandy and Tong were all stuck to me in some way or another, I knew that this was where I was meant to be.

I previously thought that what went on in the children's circle was secondary to what went on in the adult circle, but this is far from true. When children are treated with love and respect for their ability to be creative contributors to their community and the world as a whole, as a powerful force that we must think about and respect in the present, not just as "the future of leaders of our country", they take ownership of a situation. While the children's circle truly does appear chaotic to an outside observer, it is their ability to be in control of the room that makes it the most democratic of the circles.

The children's activities at Jane Addams School are not overtly political, educational, or that out of the ordinary. We play board games, do crafts, draw pictures, and have free time in the gym, swing on the swing set outside, and go sledding. The "magic" that happens in the children's circle comes out of the loving, respectful way children are treated, thought about, and talked about. What happens in the children's circle takes on the character of the creative abilities of the children who are present rather than just keeping kids occupied so they do not get in trouble.

So when I make "snack" with Joe, NeNe and Lee for all the other kids, it is because they decide what it is they want to make. I do not tell them, "add this here" or "take that there." Each kid has something to contribute, and it is through the strong personal relationships between adults and children that brings out every child's and every adult's unique contribution to the group as a whole. When new people come in to help with the children's circle, they are given the freedom and time to get to know the kids as a person to play Chutes and Ladders with and not as their leader, teacher or supervisor. Because of this experience, both the adult and the child can connect and grow.

Thursday summer trips to the Philadelphia Farm, a Community Supported Agriculture (CSA) Farm in Osceola, WI, became my time to bond with the kids. One particular experience stands out. After harvesting onions all morning, it was finally lunchtime. As I ate with Vang and his three children, Christina, his only girl, started to converse with me. This was the first day I really started connecting with her. After we ate she asked me, "Gunnar, will you push me on the swing over there?" Without hesitating or waiting for an answer, she grabbed my hand and led me over to the swing.

Once on the swing, in a tone that was ever so casual, she began to tell me about her cousin who had recently died in a car accident. The reality of her story and emotions came through as I listened to this 6-year-old girl share herself, her feelings and her understanding of death. She could not name the complex emotions involved with death. What she did understand was that her friend was dead, and, "At the funeral, there were even some people that were crying". Her conversation took me back in time four years, to my own first experience with death. Remembering that first feeling of death made Christina's story that much more of a connection between the two of us, a connection and relationship that had meaning after 10 minutes of conversation. I knew how to speak with her on a level that she dictated, not as adult to child, but as human beings, Christina and Gunnar.

This same liberation happened in my experience with algebra at Jane Addams School. As Pa Nhia came to me more and more for help with algebra, I felt inadequate as a "teacher" or "tutor", for I could not remember algebra well enough from 8th grade to explain step by step how to use the Pythagorean Theory. I had to learn algebra again, but do so in a way that involved both Pa Nhia and I. What gives life to the algebra is not that it is fun, but that we collaboratively work together as learners to create an understanding that comes from us, not a text book.

While the Founder's Lounge at the Neighborhood House is far from the most studious environment, Pa Nhia, Mary Lee, Lao, Thai, Xor, Na Cha Lee and I gladly claim it as our homework area for the night. Xor is just there to hang out with Pa Nhia and Mary Lee, which adds a little life to the room. It is not so academic anymore. As Ann and two other college students come in to help, Pa Nhia tells me, "We got a lot of work to do. Math, science, spelling, and English. Let's do math first." Mary Lee and Na Cha Lee pair up with the other college students, with Ann splitting her time between Lao and Thai. As Pa Nhia and I finish up her algebra in a little less that an hour, I see that besides Thai and Mary Lee, the other kids are done with their homework. Instead of taking off to the Youth Center with the rest of the children's circle, Na Cha Lee, Lao, and Xor stay here, occasionally drawing us all into their conversation.

Right then, NeNe walks in with her book bag. NeNe and I have a special closeness that is based on dual respect and honesty. Being one of the few African-American kids at JAS makes her experience a bit more unique. She sticks out, in her own charismatic and irreverent way adding greatly to the overall character at JAS. Tonight she calls out, "Y'all gots to help me with my homework." She was testing the waters, for she knew that Pa Nhia and I work closely together (almost always for the whole two hours), and is probably threatened to some degree by this lack of attention. NeNe likes to engage in power struggles. She continues on, "You never help me! Every time I need help, you gots to be workin' with someone else. You don't care nothin'!"

Before I could even start to respond to her, an amazing thing happened. Pa Nhia jumped in and said, "NeNe, if you just wait 5 more minutes, I'll help you with your homework, okay?" She continued, "I'll just tell you all the answers...Just kidding, just kidding, Gunnar!" Laughing as to say, "got you!" She then exclaimed, "I know, I know, that's not how we do things here." She was serious though. There was a tone of respect in her voice. I do not think this respect was for me though, but instead for the idea that learning is a process of human interaction. As I watched those two work together—Pa Nhia 13, and NeNe 8—I was struck by the beauty of what the homework group had become.

When personal relationships are an integral part of the learning environment, the wall separating teacher from student ceases to exist. Jane Addams School creates an atmosphere where education lives and where the experience of learning is real. The stories of Zoua, Christina, Mary Lee, Pa Nhia, and NeNe are only a small fraction of examples of how people of all ages interact and learn together, continually participating in an experience that liberates us all to be more fully human.

Reflecting on my ideas and experiences at Jane Addams School, I begin to understand my pursuit of the work as a part of something bigger, probably unattainable in my lifetime, but something worthy of pursuing. This pursuit forces me to be active in the world in which I live. In order to keep my life from being static; my vision must consider all people. The process of becoming fully human through loving and respecting all people is a lifelong pursuit. Even when faced with situations that are more constricting than liberating, I know no other reality.

Whether it is in a job or deciding if I should go to graduate school, I need only ask myself one question, "Can I participate in 'x' and act in a way that is compatible with what I believe?" As long as my vision is tied to the practical work that I do, the worlds that I enter, no matter how restricting, must allow me to love and respect others, even the oppressors. When I risk seeing both the oppressor and the oppressed in each and every one of us, a sense of fearlessness arises. This risk is taken by many at Jane Addams School, by college students and residents alike, and the result is freedom. A freedom that is practical, alive and real rather than theoretical or conceptual. Pursuing this freedom will guide my work for the rest of my life.

"Part of the reason that I sang at the Freedom Festival was that I wanted to educate people about the Hmong...I wanted to show that even though we are her without a country, we have talents and can contribute."

Lia Yang

Section 7
Lia Yang
Mai Chia Thao*
Terri Wilson
"Voices Sewn Together"

Mee Yang*
Terri's Journal

Lia Yang

It was 1979 when my mother passed away. My mother died because the Communists shot her. I wasn't with her. When I heard about her death I started my seven-day journey. I had to walk seven days and nights and was bitten by a snake while trying to go to her. Finally I saw my brother-in-law. He came up and asked me why it had taken me so long to get there because my mother was rotting already. My brother-in-law fell into my lap and cried. I told him, "Don't cry because I am still here." He told me how my mother had died. He said the Communists shot her as she was carrying a basket. After she was shot, she was just lying on the road.

I couldn't make it in time to see her the way I wanted to remember her. My feet hurt so much.

Before the war started, my parents were fine. They went to work in the farm while I stayed home. They would tell me to feed the pigs and roosters, get the rice to cook for dinner, cut wood so we could make a fire, and get water from the well. I would go into the forest and to a stream to get water. Older relatives helped me, but we all carried buckets of water. Mine was little, and theirs were bigger. I was ten years old then.

I remember all the things my parents taught me when I was young. They taught me how to get opium from the purple flowers—how to cut the flower in half, get the opium out of the flower, and put the opium in a jar to take home. My family would sell it to some Chinese people so we could get money to survive. Those people came to our village to buy the opium so they could take it to their country to sell to somebody else.

After the war came, many people's parents died, and family members were separated from one another. And we didn't get opium from the flowers anymore.

In my life after the war, everything was gone. Houses were destroyed, animals killed, and the opium flowers gone. I had barely anything left. We put what little was left in caves because we couldn't stay in our homes. We just ran from one village to the next. We lived wherever we could find cover—near big rocks or in caves. We lived in the forest for eight years. Each year while we waited for the bamboo to grow so we could eat it, we ate from the banana trees. That is how we ate to survive, so we could live longer.

We ran from the Communists and lived in the forest all those years. We ran for so long. We heard noises from the Communists all around us, looking for us. At night, my child would cry, so when I fed him, I had to pour a little bit of opium into his drink so he would fall asleep. Then when morning came, he would play again. But when he was too noisy I had to feed him opium. A couple times I used too much opium, and he almost died.

It was scary because I had to keep on feeding my baby opium, but he was still crying and crying, making lots of noise.

We went to Thailand by crossing the Mekong River. It took two hours to cross the river. With me was my husband and four children. The only way the Laotian people would let us cross the river was by giving them money. Each person cost fifty dollars.

When I finally got to Thailand, people told me no refugees were able to go to America and to go back to Laos. But I knew that my life in

Laos would be too hard—I hardly had a home to live in. So I said I wanted to come to America. I stayed in Thailand for two years.

Before we came to America, people in Thailand warned us of the big monsters in America that were going to eat us. People also said that if we went to America we would marry dogs. But I said, "Whatever might happen, monsters or not, I still want to go to America."

You see, in Thailand I was so very poor. My shirts were all ripped, my chest exposed, my dresses too short, and I had to carry my baby on my back. An American in the refugee camp took a picture of me. That is when I thought, "I will leave Thailand." The Americans saw that I was so poor and told me to go to America because my life would be better.

There would be no war.

But my husband didn't want to go to America. I told him if he didn't want to come to America he would be by himself, because I had made up my mind that, no matter what, I would go to America. I wanted to support my children so they would not be poor like me. My husband thought about it for a day and night, crying a lot. The next morning he said that we should all go to America. So we added our names to the list to go to America.

I haven't seen any monsters in America, so I realize that was just a lie. For ten years I have been living here and I haven't seen any monsters at all.

Nobody has married the American dogs either.

When I came to America, even though I was poor and didn't have any clothing, I did everything to keep my children alive. I taught them what Americans do; taught them what life was like in America. I told myself to just throw away the old life, don't keep it or carry it with me. Start with a new life.

When I moved into the apartments on the West Side of St. Paul, my relative went to Neighborhood House. She kept telling me to come. That was before Jane Addams School began.

I like Jane Addams School because I get help with English and learn how to write. There are people who help me, and now my life is going well. Learning how to become a citizen, taking the citizenship test, English—all of those things go on at Jane Addams School.

◻

I have three daughters, and two of them are married. One is still living with me. My sons are all still living with me. I teach my boys how to tell stories, sing, play the qeej and other bamboo instruments. They learn about American culture too. I am their first mother, and the people at JAS are their other mothers. They teach my children about life and what it is like. They learn from the teachers. My children gain a lot from the experiences at Jane Addams School.

When I was five or six years old, I learned some traditional Hmong songs. I kept them in my heart. At the Freedom Festival, I sang these songs. I wanted the Americans to know that we have songs to sing. All my friends at Jane Addams School have helped me, and I wanted them to know me, to hear what my life back then was like.

Now that my boys saw me sing at the Freedom Festival, they want me to sing for them; and they would like to learn to sing, too. Every night I sing to my boys and teach them how to sing and tell Hmong stories.

> A long time ago there was an orphan boy whose parents had died. He was very young, but his uncles sent him to the fields to feed the cows and take them for walks. When he saw a Chinese person go by, he sang a song about his life, about how he was an orphan who didn't have any parents, about how every day he was sent to the fields to follow the cows.

Every night I teach my sons how to tell these stories, but while we tell them, we sing. Even though they are stories, we sing them.

There is so much of what happened back in Laos in my heart. I remember everything I did back then. The way I lived keeps coming back to me. When I think of the things I went through, I have a hard time learning. I am not sure I can learn anything else. I have so much trouble concentrating. Everyone is helping me but because of my thinking of life back then I have had a hard time. I just wish that I could learn like when I was young, that I could learn everything easily.

Before, I only heard about freedom, but now I am free to do things. The Bible says there is freedom, so I am happy about that. I became a Christian in 1979 in Laos. Christianity made me think a lot and feel better too. I became a Christian because I didn't want to dwell on the hard times. I wanted to leave them behind me.

Mai Chia Thao*

My name is Mai Chia Thao. I was born in Laos, but I don't know what year.

While I was growing up, my family and I lived in many villages. We were forced to travel a great deal because of the war. My parents died when I was about four or five years old due to the strain of constant traveling. My parents were sensitive to extreme weather and some-times it was exhaustingly hot. I had seven siblings, six of whom died along the way. After my parents died, my younger brother and I lived with my uncle who was a soldier in the "Secret War." I was married in Laos when I was about 16. Three years after I was married, we had a son, Gaolee.

---

* The name Mai Chia Thao and all other names used in this story are pseudonyms.

The Communist troops were beginning to invade the villages looking for soldiers who had fought in the "Secret War." Since my family relied on my uncle for support, we knew that we had to move out of Laos. My uncle, and distant uncles and cousins whom we called grandfathers, escaped first. Then some grandfathers came back to help us escape.

There were a thousand people in our group who were escaping to Thailand. We had to sneak our way through the jungle at night to avoid Communist troops. At this time, my son was five years old. There were many dangers in the jungle. There were traps set by the Communist soldiers throughout the jungle. A person who was traveling with us almost set off a bomb. The noise from the bomb would have alerted the soldiers to our whereabouts, and they would have found, and killed us. The Communist troops also camouflaged themselves in the jungle and then jumped out and attacked. Once we were ambushed but managed to escape. One person died in the shootout.

Another danger we encountered was the flooding from the Mekong River. The water would create swamps that had quicksand. If you stepped in the water and sunk to your waist or shoulders, there was no way to escape. We spent 21 days in the jungle without rest. There are small towns and villages in the jungle, but it was not safe to stop in them because the Communist soldiers often stopped to rest at these villages. When we got to the Mekong River, some kindhearted boat people brought us across the river to Thailand. We lived in a refugee camp in Thailand for three or four years waiting for sponsorship from a family in order to come to the United States.

Finally, we were sponsored by some relatives. I remember my thoughts on the plane. I kept thinking over and over,

"Where am I going? Why am I leaving my country? It is sad that I am leaving my country."

We came directly to St. Paul from Thailand in December 1988.

I had never seen snow before. When I walked outside the airport, I thought that there was a lot of salt on the ground. At first, I was scared to go outside because it was so white, and I thought it was dangerous to walk on the snow and ice. It made me sad because it was so different. I like living in Minnesota now because I have many relatives here, but at that time I was afraid.

After we came to St. Paul, my husband and I went to school for four months at the International Institute on Como Avenue. It was very difficult because we had no one to care for our children and we had to take buses in the winter to get there. My husband suffers from many health problems and cannot work. I did not have a formal education in Laos. After my parents died, I could not afford to go to school. I had to work and try to support myself.

I now have seven children, and they can speak some English. My oldest son goes to high school in Mankato. He lives with some relatives there. We wanted him to get away from the city and its bad influences so that he could concentrate on school. I do not get to see him very much.

I come to the Jane Addams School because I want to study and learn how to speak English. I am trying my hardest to learn English, but it is very difficult for me.

Terri Wilson

To me, freedom is this kind of internal compass.

This idea goes back to my growing up.

Every person's family and upbringing and place has its own culture, but we don't usually think of that. We usually say, "Oh, I don't have a culture because my ethnicity has been lost or diluted or changed or mixed." Part of my most easily defined culture is that my family is very Scottish, and there are some things that come with that that are still there after so many years. It includes stubbornness, determination, and a lot of family-centered things. The main thing with my family is that family responsibility is a big part of who we are. I think there's an important emphasis in my family on really caring for people: caring outside of yourself, being a loving person, a good friend.

There would be no way for me not to pass this on to my own kids because it's so much a part of me. I want so many things for children in general, and my children specifically. I want them to feel like they're creative, independent, loving, grounded people.

☐

I think my life is very dominated by family. It has definitely shaped who I am in a lot of important ways. It's given me certain values about responsibility and being with the people you love.

I have such huge admiration and love for my parents. I think the way that we were brought up, most of the ways, I really agree with. They encouraged us to be independent, which I think is so important—to learn to defend yourself and your beliefs, to have a sort of internal compass of who you are and what you want—rather than being shaped by situations. Both my sister and I have this sense of "This is who we are."

My sister and I were raised in a safe and challenging space. We grew up on boy scout camps, and we were not expected to fall into roles. We weren't trained as "girls." Because there were just two of us girls, there was no idea that "this is what the boys do and this is what the girls do." Instead, it was, "This is what we do because this is what my father does, and we're going along with it." And that was good—most of the time.

When my sister and I thought we were getting too old to have baby-sitters, my parents did the smartest thing ever—they would pay us to baby-sit ourselves. Something like five cents an hour. If they had left us home accidentally, or if we had been left with the baby-sitter, then we would have had no internal responsibility for our actions. We could have blamed the baby-sitter, saying, "Oh, the baby-sitter has to make us behave." Or we could have said, "You just left us, so we didn't have to behave." They would leave everything for us—saying, "This is dinner, and this is where we're going to be, and we'll be home at this time." It was so smart because they located the center of responsibility within us, not in something external. It's one of the best things I learned.

My father's only rule when we were growing up was, "Justify your actions." I could do whatever I wanted; I never had any rules, and I was never grounded or had curfew. It was just that I had to battle it out and justify to him if I wanted to stay out late. I had to justify it.

My family moved around quite a bit. Moving gives you a longing for a sense of place. I think that's been a major love-loss that I've had in my life—not having that continuity of place where you know the people of a community, where you have these longtime friends. I think that's why I'm so close to my sister, because she's one of the few people who has been with me consistently throughout my life. She understands the fact that I'm both uncomfortable and very comfortable in the city, and that some times I just have bad days with cement.

Every time I moved was a turning point for me, just because of the whole process of deciding what about myself I wanted to keep and what about the new place I wanted to let in.

I was forced to adapt to new situations and to be more self-aware. In my teen years, I often found myself swept up in a lot of currents, and I had to be aware of what about myself I didn't want to lose.

Moving strengthened my extended family, because everyone moved around so much that we always wanted to come back to each other. I feel like my grandparents' farm and my other grandparents' land was home because it was the only thing that never changed. There's this saying that I sent to my mom that says, "My home is in my mother's eyes." It's the sense that you come home to your family, not really to any one place.

My grandparents have a streak of old-fashionedness. It includes a strong work ethic, and the value of being in one place and doing good work with family. It comes from both sets of my grandparents, and I guess being from the rural Midwest. There's an emphasis on land and "honest, decent work" and a "sense of being in one place." It's something old fashioned about living in a small town and just being there. My grandfather died a year ago—my mother's father—and I remember the day of the visitation there was this huge snowstorm. Being in a rural place, traveling was difficult. But at the visitation there were still people lined up outside the house, out the door, and it was amazing for me to see what happens when you spend your whole life in a place where people love you. My grandfather was a fixture, an essential part of the community. I felt this strong sense of community, accountability and place in their small town. I was inspired.

The experience of living in a small town has shaped my view of community work—the fact that the personalities of people and doing things are such vital parts of how you do work. I see the importance of being part of a small community where you work in the community and you see the people everyday. Things just sort of happen naturally.

I realize more and more as I have contact with people who are from other cultures, that being part of the rural Midwest is my culture. I wasn't aware of this until I came to Minneapolis from rural Wisconsin, and then I thought, "Yeah, I guess I do have a rural background." I have a different perspective on how people interact with each other. It is a sense that being anonymous is not good.

Freedom is having the awareness and the sense of urgency to do something.

When I was younger, I was terribly shy, so quiet. I remember third grade when I had just moved to a new school, they had a guidance counselor who came to our class to do different things. One of the activities was that every week it would be a new person's turn, and everyone in the class would write one good thing about that person on a piece of paper, and then they'd all send it to the person. Ideally each of us received 25 good things. But no one knew me—I had just moved there—so I got 25 little pieces of paper that said "quiet." And some of them were spelled wrong—"quite."

I hated being shy, because I knew that wasn't really me. It wasn't me in my family. It wasn't how I was inside. In sixth or seventh grade I purposefully joined everything that would get me to be un-shy. I started a middle-school debate team, and I debated on the high school level. I joined speech and drama and student council. I aggressively put myself in situations that were uncomfortable for me. It helped shape my personality. I was involved with a community of people who were more creative and vocal. I took my place in a supportive group of people. It definitely helped me be more vocal and more political.

People are defined by physical size and appearance. I'm small, young looking, and very blonde. There is a whole bunch of stereo-types that go with all of that. At work, people think, "You're just a kid," and they don't take you seriously. As a student, you don't have the trappings that make you professional or that give you the credentials to approach the academic world. It's difficult. I have evolved as a super-articulate woman, which really isn't me, to face particular situations.

❑

I was just floating around in the Philosophy Department at the University of Minnesota. I love ideas and the muscle involved in grappling with them. At the same time, I was frustrated that none of the ideas seemed to apply to the "real world." When I started doing my work at Jane Addams School, it was a seamless fit—I began doing philosophy in a community setting.

On one level of my Jane Addams School experience, I am a member of our community. I am one of the people from different cultures who are doing things together. And this is challenging. It would be easy for me to be with a group of people from Wisconsin or a group of college students. It's much more challenging to be with people who don't speak the same language, who come from different cultures, and who are relating across differences. It's also much more powerful. The whole experience is education in the purest sense of learning. That's what really grabbed me, what caught me about Jane Addams School.

The idea of doing education in a way that encourages community participation—doing education democratically, has given me focus. Jane Addams School has given me a sense of, "This is my work." I have such ownership. This is what I do. This is me. This is how I want to continue to live my life: having my life interact with my work.

Working at Jane Addams School has made academic learning more meaningful. I am interested in academic subjects because I can apply them to what I do. I am using academic language and academic subjects as tools for understanding Jane Addams School. Too often people use their community work to describe a theory they already have; they see the community experience as a means. In my learning I realize that community work is an end in itself. When people describe the work that they're doing to further their own theories but don't view the people and the lives involved as valuable, then they use people's lives as a means to further their own academic ends. It seems wrong to me. Academic theory is one thing, but people are worthy of our respect. Their lives, their struggles are complete.

After you've been at Jane Addams School, you get to know people as people. Jane Addams School is not an "example of something or a study of something." I experience Jane Addams School as a conglomeration of all these people I know, and they are people, not immigrants preparing for the citizenship exam. I've learned that people are full of grace. Full of dignity.

Freedom means taking the responsibility to create freedom for others.

Recently, we had a cultural exchange about music—instruments and singing. It was classic Jane Addams School—seven o'clock: everyone who was supposed to bring an instrument wasn't there yet. Everything was kind of disorganized. But it showed the strength of knowing people and of trusting each other. No one seemed overly concerned about the lack of organization. After a couple of minutes, all these children went scurrying off to call their parents or went to other people's houses to get instruments, and the high school students ran over to a nearby house that they knew had a trumpet. It was like a car commercial— nothing to education in fifteen minutes.

At the beginning of the exchange, Nick was standing up there facilitating, and the only instrument we had was my flute that I hadn't played in about ten years. Then all of a sudden, people started spilling in, bringing their instruments. There was this feeling that everyone contributed to making it happen. I think Nick did a wonderful job because he was so patient, waiting for things to happen naturally. It illustrated that education is about holding the space for things to happen; if you pause and keep the space open, pretty soon people will step into it with their creativity and the things that they've brought. So we had children, high school and college students, and adults stepping into the space. And it was so great because the entire room was filled with laughter.

This embodied Jane Addams School for me. I want to be doing something where people are stepping out, being creative, being a part of something. And when I see it happening, like that night, it's meaningful to me. Some people would have walked in and seen chaos, but because we truly believe that this is our work, and because we know and trust each other, we see the power of it all.

Another thing I saw in that situation was the power of creating an intergenerational space. That night Nick just said, "OK everyone, we're going to start." And because the parents were in the room, the children were instantaneously quiet. And that never happens. Fifteen minutes later, when the parents left, it just wouldn't happen. It was such a unique space, such a unique cultural space. There was such a safe feeling, and the children could be like, "Yeah, I'm learning about this and that's my parent over there. We're learning together."

One other thing that happened was with Judy, who would almost never speak Hmong, especially with adults around. When she first started coming, she would never want to translate, never do anything like that. She would listen in Hmong and answer in English, listen in Hmong and answer in English. But that night, she wanted Yang to sing, so across this crowded room full of people she was yelling to him in Hmong, "Koj yuav tsum tau hais kws txhiaj, koj yuav tsum tau hais kws tshiaj."* It was an amazing thing to see. First, to see her have the confidence to speak out in such a huge group of people. And second, having the confidence to actually use her Hmong. That made me really happy.

Another moment at Jane Addams School: One night I came in late, and everyone had formed learning pairs already. I had all of the materials for the paj ntaub project, so I sat out in the hallway to work on it. Children were racing around, and they would kind of slow down when they saw what I was doing. It was just this steady pouring in of children, and they were all gathered around me in this loose crazy circle. The girls, and even the boys, sat down and started pulling thread out of the bag. It was this amazing, chaotic, beautiful thing. There were children and bright threads and material. People were helping each other and older children were showing their younger brothers and sisters how to sew. It was such an incredible, creative moment, and they were so excited about it.

You had the sense that education is just about creating a good space, and then children could come in and be really interested and involved. They were learning something that they cared about. It was really good.

One of my favorite stories about Jane Addams School comes from the Freedom Festival. For me, the best thing about the Freedom Festival, the best moment—and there were lots of good moments—was seeing Lia sing. It was incredible, especially knowing Lia so well—knowing how quiet she is, how reserved she is, and how sad she is. To see her get up and sing these amazingly beautiful songs, to be able to reclaim her voice, was so powerful. She would always say that she was the best singer in Laos because she could sing louder than the waterfalls. When she said this, I could see how she had been sort of worn down here because she hadn't had a place to do that. There wasn't a public place where she could be herself. It made me cry, seeing her sing that day.

I remember one time Mai Lor and I were working on writing. She would write something in Hmong, and then I would try to make sense

---

* "You must sing, you must sing."

of it. We were talking about friendship, and then she wrote "Koj yog kuv tus phooj ywg thiab kuv hlub koj heev."* As I was trying to puzzle it out, she was laughing at me so much. When I found out what it said, it was just so beautiful.

Seeing the importance of creativity has illustrated to me that real freedom is not in opposition to external forces.

The best thing about Jane Addams School is that it involves such a diverse range of ages, experiences, and people. Simultaneously a space is being created for you to be creative. John has created this educational space for me where I can be a creative student, where I as a young person am given the freedom to do good work. A free space. But simultaneously I'm also put in the role where I'm becoming an "older" person, a more experienced person, at Jane Addams School. So as the space is being created for me, I'm also creating that space for other people—for new college students, new children, new residents or parents who come in.

I think that's how education becomes democratic. When you have this beautiful accountability for educating people at the same time that you're being educated. It goes back to where the authority and power comes from. It isn't external. In a usual school, all of the authority

* "You are my friend, and I love you very much."°

and the responsibility for organizing things is located externally, so it's really easy to drift off, to drift away. You don't claim responsibility for creating that space at the same time that you're in that space. If you say you're creating a democratic space, and you're the one creating and the people are the ones participating, it doesn't work as well as it should. I think that's one of the major things I've learned, that if you're creating a space for the students involved, and they're not at the same time creating spaces of their own, it's much less democratic. If students in the group don't take responsibility for creating the space for other students or creating the space for their own work, then the sense that you're really sharing power and sharing creativity doesn't exist.

In democratic education, you don't jump in and organize the space; you jump in and hold the space. And silence and pauses and waiting are much more important than speaking or doing.

"Voices sewn together into a quilt about us"

By Terri Wilson

The Paj Ntaub (literally meaning "flower cloth") sewing project was a collaborative sewing project between women and their children of all ages, between distinct cultures and backgrounds. Every person participating made a small piece of the project, and these pieces were brought together in a quilt, a mural of fabric, representing the relationships, cultures and work of the Jane Addams School for Democracy. This particular conversation arose out of one of the thousands of informal conversations that occur between people working together. This conversation was about sewing, passing down skills between generations.

This project also explored the idea of relationships. The relationships at JAS, especially the ones that have developed over years, are powerful because they have occurred across cultures, languages, families and the usual lines of generations. This should be a new American flag. Bright colors, different patterns, children learning to stitch around the edges. Stitching that holds things together. Shao's piece has the American flag sewn into it, as well as the names of all the people at JAS who she works with.

The colors fall out of my bag. I find strands woven into my clothing afterwards. And I notice that part of my hand is rough with my needle's mistakes. I have always been terrible at sewing. I was afraid that the machine would eat my hands, and I liked to play outside much more than threading needles. Countless women in my family have been sewing countless quilts and I inadvertently lost the ability to do it. Maybe it was because there was no definite need for the skill, or because my mother lost the ability to explain why she thought it was important, but I never learned.

> This sewing project formed a space where the talents, strengths, and hands of people creating are recognized as public voices.

Mee Yang*

I was born in Laos on April 10, 1962. I grew up, became married and had a son. My husband was a soldier when the Communists began raiding our country. In the aftermath of the official war, we were forced to flee for the relative safety of Thailand. From where we lived in Laos, it was a month's journey to the Mekong River, the border of Thailand.

My husband and I traveled with our grandparents and many other refugees from our community. I carried my 2 and _-year-old son, as well as the rice that would sustain us through the journey, on my back. We could carry with us only rice and each other. My grandparents were older, slower, and could not carry rice, so at times we lived on roots found within the jungle.

The other large groups of friends, relatives and others that were running immediately before and after our group were hunted down and indiscriminately killed by Communists soldiers, who came invading and cornering us faster than we could escape. These soldiers knew that we were hiding somewhere in the jungle, but they were not able to find us. We ran by night and hid ourselves by day. To kill us, they poisoned all the fresh water and simply waited.

We were only saved because a family member who had escaped managed to warn us of the poison. We waited in stillness beside the stagnant water, hiding from the soldiers, without water for cooking or drinking, living off of the drops of water that collected in green leaves. For the last two days before we reached the river, we no longer had anything to eat and could not stop moving. We staggered lost through the dark, with nothing to follow except the fading footprints of those who had died before us.

Once we came to the river, we had to cross it on roughly fashioned bamboo rafts. Our raft was so full, with six people, that we sank until the water came up to our chests and we had to strain to keep our balance. I could not swim, and I had to hold my child up above the water as we went.

As we crossed the river, the current swept different groups of people into the small inlets of Thailand. Our group was fortunate to fall into an inlet occupied by the Thai army. The group behind us drifted into an inlet controlled by Thai rebels who beat them and took any possessions they might still have. They shot above the group, shouting, frightening. My relative was in this group and was holding a gun— without firing— trying to protect his family. When he wouldn't drop his weapon, they shot him through the forehead and pushed his body into the river. The survivors, beaten, eventually found our group.

The Thai army, who was charged with helping us, was also hostile, repeatedly shooting their weapons above our heads, laughing as the shells rained down upon us. Many people, frightened, would scream and cry as the empty shells struck them because they thought they were being killed. The soldiers then took us to the Ban Vinai refugee camp.

By the time we arrived at the camp, my son was so hungry that he could no longer cry. All I had left was one earring, which I traded for a small handful of rice. As I fed him the rice, he began to cry.

We settled roughly into life at the refugee camp in Thailand. We were not permitted to leave; barbed-wire fences surrounded the camp. If we attempted to go outside the barbed wire, we were beaten. I would remain here for the next 13 years. My first daughter was born in the camp on October 10, 1985. My second son was born on December 23, 1986.

The camp was 9 miles square, crossed by rows and rows of shelters. Each shelter was shared by four or five families. Once every week, each person received two handfuls of rice and a 5-gallon pail of water. Occasionally there were teachers, but my children and I taught ourselves to read and write.

Within a year of coming to the refugee camp, my husband returned to Laos as a soldier to help liberate the country and reclaim our homes from the Communist occupation. He was captured by Communist soldiers in the third year that he was away. I would hear later of what happened.

> He was tortured for information. The soldiers had a large burlap bag, the kind that usually holds 100 pounds of rice. Tied within the heavy burlap bad, he could not move and saw only shadows as the soldiers beat him with thick wood, stabbed him again and again.
>
> When there was nothing left but a little life within his body, they tumbled him out of the bag and unto the floor. His left arm was broken. Taking a knife, they cut deeply across his forehead, so that his skin fell open lying almost gently across his eyes. They poured salt on his wounds. His death was not quick. To prove that he had been tortured, they sliced his ear from his body to give to their general. His body was thrown into the river. The soldiers had tortured him, trying to get information about who was controlling the efforts to free Laos.
>
> He died silently, without betrayal.

After my husband's death, I began the long process of coming to the United States. I had no sponsors, no relatives. I eventually discovered that my sister was living in California. My oldest son did not want to go to the United States because we did not speak English, and he feared that we would not be able to communicate or survive in a strange place. He remained in Thailand while my other children and I came to California and eventually to Minnesota. On the bus ride from California to Minnesota, I did not know how to find food or even ask for help. We lived off the juice that was sold on the bus.

My son is now living illegally in Thailand.* He is twenty, married and has a son of his own. We write every month, and I help them by sending money whenever I can. He and his family can no longer come to the United States because of a change in the immigration laws.

My sister and my mother are living in Fresno, California. My father and my brother are described as "those who are eating leaves," escaping captivity by hiding in the forests of Laos. I am remarried now and have three more children. My hope is that my children can graduate from high school, even college, and find successful jobs.

For years, while I waited in the camp in Thailand, I thought and dreamed that I could come to the United States, become more educated, and go to work. Because I cannot speak English well, I cannot find a job, cannot go to school. I am trying to learn English and pass my citizenship exam; since the Jane Addams School began, I have missed only one night. I am very afraid of what will happen when my welfare ends because I do not know how my family and I will survive. I only need more time—time to learn English, learn to drive, study for my citizenship exam, be able to work.

The only thing I need is time.

---

*Many Hmong refugees, fearful of resettling in a strange land and hopeful that one day they can return to a liberated Laos, have settled illegally in Thailand. Approximately 15,000 Hmong are currently seeking refuge in Wat Tham Krabok, a Buddhist temple in Central Thailand. Occupying roughly 40 acres on the back of the temple property, these people live in constant fear of deportation by the Thai government. (St. Paul Pioneer Press, April, 1995)

Journal Entry by Terri Wilson After Recording Mee's* Story

fast thoughts after the telling of a story - april 1997

these broken glass events ease off her too smoothly.
i want to fill the spaces between me and her, between
her words and downward glances, between that place –
that time – and this, with anger – something heavy
and solid and flat. i want to be water or rage...
some action besides this slow silence, the paralysis
of beaten down emotion and empathy. (she doesn't
wear me down... the story – it's delicate neutrality
erodes me away... so that i slump down and cannot
speak.)   but i am not so well varnished –
this story doesn't peacefully fall from my lips with
the practiced ease of what is familiar from necessity.
this water breaks me into slow sharp pieces. i am
splintered and jangled. salt and broken wood. and
there is no ease of escape... silence cannot carve out
again what has been given – when you ask a question,
you make a covenant to honor its response. i splinter
upon myself, my inability to conceive-understand -
accept the answers to my questions.   i stumble and
fall into all the places she has learned to walk easily
through. that she has stopped lingering in, fled,
hardened, forgiven.   this act (or inaction) of
listening -passive- bits into skin i didn't know i had.
catches in places of my throat that make no sound.
(cannot protest or truly hurt)   this story doesn't
hurt me... that wouldn't be my hurt. i ache
because the story curves steadily into parts of me –
impressions – experiences – emotions – i didn't know
existed.

and these uncomforts, small and unsettled, will not ease with the simple retelling of a story. any story would fail if it enabled the storyteller to forget in its telling. it is a remembrance, a changing, a refraction, to relate to someone else's frame of reference. the best stories should evolve for different audiences — the teller (almost inevitably?) makes alterations, for fit, impact, effect. but all without altering the essential truth: the events, the patterns of language — that give it her truth, her experience.   and you cannot breathe people as air. people's experiences, once taken in, accepted, cannot be easily exhaled. people get tangled up in places inside. to attempt to feel, know, hold unto, anything of someone; i must gasp in — commit every cell to feel this listening, this holding in — not breathing, the rigid point of salt.   to justify, to feel right, in my emotional response to this story, it cannot simply pass through my experience — it has to be more to me than one breath in a bigger process.   i have to take it all, be committed to responding to it — even though this response may be silent, halted, stumbling.   i am, and should be, only a small part of this process... but the story should be (or become) a part of me.

"Growing up, I heard many stories of
my parents' journey out of Laos."

Kong Yang Thao

Section 8
Nick Longo
Kou Yang
Kong Yang Thao
Kai Lee

JOYCE YAMAMOTO

"All actual life is encounter."
Martin Buber

Nick Longo

Whenever I traveled in the car with my mother I would always sit behind her and put my hand on her shoulder while she drove. As long as I can remember, I would always do this. I think it was a way to connect with her, to be supportive of her.

Family, Community, and Politics

I grew up in Yonkers, New York. Yonkers is a working class suburb of New York City. Very ethnic Italian and Irish. Most of my friends growing up were Italian-American, and many of their parents were immigrants.

My family lived in an apartment building, in a small two-bedroom apartment. My two older sisters and I shared one room and my parents were in the other room. My mother's mother lived one block away and my father's parents lived a block away also. I basically grew up with my mother, my older sisters and my two grandmothers raising me. My father worked two jobs. He was an insurance salesman and a local councilman for Yonkers. With those two jobs he probably worked a 70-hour week.

When I was eight years old we moved into a house. It was pretty close to our old apartment, but it was a lot different. The apartment was more urban. There was a park right there where people would hang out. When I lived in the apartment it was much more intergenerational. Kids of all different ages would play together. Once I moved to the house, it seemed like kids of the same age played together. There was more space, but in a more suburban setting. Everyone had backyards.

There were two things that I knew growing up—politics and the Mets. I could talk to any adult, anybody about those two topics. Some days, I would read the newspaper for hours and learn the baseball averages of all the players for the week. When my father and I watched the games I knew everyone's batting average. I walked down the block swinging a make-believe baseball bat or throwing a make-believe ball. I was really into sports. I loved to play.

Both of my parents had a huge influence on my love of politics, community, and public life. My mother was president of the PTA and my father was on the city council for sixteen years so I just grew up with it. Anywhere I went people would know me as my father's son.

They used to yell out, "There's Nick Longo's son Nicky Longo!"

When you're a local politician everything is so much closer to home. If people needed a tree cut down they would call my house, if people had a problem with the snowplows not plowing their street they would call my house. My father gave out his home number so people were always calling about whatever problems they had.

I grew up going door to door with my father. During campaign time, it was the only time I could see my father. I went with him at night, ringing people's doorbells, seeing what was going on in the neighborhood. I really learned a lot about politics just being with him.

When I was young, Yonkers was involved in a really controversial case involving low-income housing, and my father was at the center of it. At one point there were death threats made, and we had 24-hour police protection. When my father voted a way that the people in my neighborhood really disagreed with, parents at my school told their kids not to talk to me or play with me. I could see how issues really ignite. There's a lot of anger in people. That was when I was in 8th grade. The whole experience shaped a lot of my political views, and my views about public life. In a divisive issue, I think people have to figure out ways to talk to each other and channel anger in the right way. I saw a lot of mob mentality. It's weird doing so much work around democracy when I think about that time because I saw firsthand some dangers of democracy when people don't see people as people.

> "We have forgotten that [democracy] has to be enacted anew in every generation, in every year, in the living relations of person to person, in all social forms and institutions."

> *John Dewey*

Culture and Traditions

"A man doesn't say as much but when he says something, he really means it!"

My father believed in an Italian kind of masculinity. His father was born in Italy and came over by himself when he was sixteen. My dad's mom was born in the United States but she was part of an ethnic Italian family. Her parents were born in Italy and spoke in Italian around the house. My father grew up in this really Italian household. His father was a carpenter and the idea of success was the American dream of having your child get a white-collar job and speak English. So my grandparents never wanted my father to learn Italian and they also didn't want him to do any kind of hard labor. They thought if he learned to do that stuff then he might chose to do that rather than go to college. He picked up some Italian but his parents really didn't want him to. Though his father was a carpenter, he didn't learn any of that trade.

My father's original name was Vito Nicholas Longo. It was an Italian tradition to call your child by their middle name, so he went by Nicholas. But his name on the birth certificate was Vito Nicholas. When he was in 2nd grade his teacher wouldn't call him Nicholas because his first name was Vito. My grandma had to go down and change his name officially on the birth certificate because of that teacher. So his name became Nicholas Vito. And that is my name too.

I was briefly Nicholas Cosmo Longo, because my grandfather's name was Cosmo. But then my father called the hospital when my mother was still there with me and said, "I want a junior!" so I became Nicholas Vito Longo.

My mother's parents were both born in the United States. Her father died when she was an infant, and her mother raised her. After I got involved in Jane Addams School, I started investigating my past. Her grandparents, my great-grandparents, were from Ireland. They were in love but their families didn't want them to marry each other. They couldn't get married in Ireland so they came to the United States to get married.

On Christmas Eve my family always has seven different kinds of fish. It's an old Italian tradition. I think it's from the Bible. For Easter, we always put eggs in our shoes. The Easter Bunny puts eggs in your shoes while you are sleeping. We used to do huge Sunday dinners. That is part of the Italian tradition. The whole family would come together in the basement. My grandparents had this huge house but everything was in the basement. They wanted to preserve what they worked so hard for, so we ate and socialized in the basement. My father grew up in that house and yet there were rooms he had never been in.

I think the strongest traditions are the values passed down from generation to generation. Who I am is a product of my parents, and a product of their parents, and so on. I want to teach my children to respect people. To see people as people. To not look past people. Or look through people. To struggle to love people. Children need to be critical thinkers, and recognize some of the contradictions in life; be more aware. I will definitely pass down the values, but I don't know which of the traditions I will pass down. As traditions and cultures get fragmented, the harder it is to keep the symbolic things alive. When my parents got married my father was Italian, my mother was French, Irish, German, Hungarian. We kept more of the Italian traditions but we weren't an all Italian-American family. If I marry someone who is not Italian, French, Irish, German, and Hungarian, some of the symbolic traditions will be harder. But the values of respecting and loving your friends and family, the way you treat other people, will get passed to them. It seems like a long way off right now; what I would teach my children...

For a big part of my childhood, both my grandmothers raised me. I never had a babysitter in my life. I would always just go over to one of my grandmothers' houses or one of them would come to my house. I remember my father's mother was a real storyteller. She was a real fiery Italian woman. If I ever came home after one of the kids in the neighborhood had picked on me, she'd go running out there right after the kid and yell. She'd get involved. And the kids didn't mess with her. She was a tough woman. My other grandma originally spoke German. She had had a really hard life. One of her children had passed away, and another passed away when she was older. She was a strong woman.

I was at Jane Addams, and we were talking in a Cultural Exchange on the topic of "why American's put their elderly in nursing homes." That touched me. It made me think of some of the things we do within American culture. I thought of how when my grandma got older she had Alzheimers, and she wanted to go into a nursing home. She was at a point where she needed that care. My mother took a job at that nursing home so she could spend a lot of her time with my grandmother. It was difficult when both my grandmas passed away. I was fifteen years old when one died and sixteen when the other one died.

> "I am enlightened by the things I learn working with people in action."
>
> *Myles Horton*

Education and Freedom

I went to Catholic school all my life, from pre-kindergarten through college. I think I still have funny feelings about it. I am still not at peace with what that means. I don't really agree with the way I was educated in Catholic school. I remember my 4th grade teacher had this sentence on the board and anyone who got into trouble would have to write it:

> I must do what I am told, when I am told, by whom I am told whether I like it or not.

This was the culture of the school at the time. In college, I rebelled against that whole system of authority. I wanted to find ways that education could be more liberating.

Going away to college, living on my own and meeting some amazing people really shaped who I am. I made good friends, and got involved in community work and service-learning. There was a new program at our school my junior year where you could major and minor in public service. One quarter I took three service-learning classes by chance, and loved them. Before that, I was really into political science theory, which was more abstract. This was a chance to do hands-on work. I wanted to change the world and this was a way to do it. During college, I think I became more thoughtful about life and the way I wanted to live my life. My friends and I were really committed to trying to make the world a better place and it was just what we did.

I am not a big fan of "the larger American culture" whatever that might mean. Since I have been working at the Center for Democracy and Citizenship, I have seen more of the democratic possibilities of American traditions which I probably didn't see before. But I can't help but be critical of our consumer society, which is probably our greatest cultural export. Living here, I am part of those assumptions and that society. At the same time I try to be more mindful, and try not to be a part of it. Instead, I stay on the margins and figure out ways of resistance.

I originally moved to Minnesota because of the work at the Center for Democracy and Citizenship. I came to study at the Humphrey Institute of Public Affairs, but my passion was the link between universities and communities: universities becoming resources for communities and seeing the community as part of the university's learning.

JOYCE YAMAMOTO

"Let us dare, despite all, to trust."

Martin Buber

Relationships and Jane Addams School

When I first went to Jane Addams School I didn't know what a Hmong person was. I had never met a Hmong person. I didn't really think much about immigration. Before, I didn't think about intergenerational relationships and what that meant. All these things are things I have learned just over the last few years at Jane Addams.

The reason I am involved in Jane Addams School is because of the community. I love the people, and the whole way Jane Addams School is done—the Jane Addams School way of doing things. It honors people, gives people the space to be creative, to do things. The whole structure of the school allows the cultivation of relationships, and for things to happen organically. I was going to Jane Addams originally because of the university-community partnership, but along the way I have learned so many things and now I can't imagine what my life would be like right now if I didn't go to Jane Addams School. All the things I do relate to Jane Addams School.

One good example to explain the way things happen at Jane Addams

School is Gunnar's new homework group. It emerged out of the Children's Circle. It wasn't like we did a "needs assessment" and found out the kids had homework they had to get done by a certain time so we should hire someone to manage it. Instead, Gunnar was spending time in the Children's Circle, the kids started to bring homework and he started working with them on it. The next thing you know, he started going to Neighborhood House on other days besides Mondays and Wednesdays, just sitting around with the kids doing homework.

They can be really honest with him—"Oh, this homework is two weeks late"—because they know he is not going to judge them. The organic way that this product—the Homework Group—came about is amazing! With Jane Addams School, it is not so much what we're doing, but the way we're doing it.

For me, a lot of the meaning of Jane Addams School comes from the friendships, especially for the college students. We've spent so much time at Jane Addams School, discussing Jane Addams, and talking about lives in relation to it. I met Terri at Jane Addams and a huge part of our relationship is Jane Addams School. Because of that I can really see the different elements of her. I don't have to separate "Oh, this is what I do at work, this is what I do at home." It is more complete. Each night to look over and see Terri working with people, and then be able to talk about—even on our drive home—what happened that night. It's an amazing way to experience life together. To have that partnership with a person has been amazing.

Before Jane Addams School, I didn't have much experience being with children. I was the youngest child, and I really don't have younger cousins. Many of the older boys in the Children's Circle have taught me how to be with children. I just love it now when I walk into Neighborhood House and there is Meng, Joseph, Vilai, Lee, and Chou. All these kids come running up to me and are so excited. I get to pick them up and hear about their day. I think those experiences in the hallway—before we actually start at 7 o'clock—are what Jane Addams School is about. And that's something we probably don't talk about.

In the Adult Circle, I am able to communicate much better with people than when I first started. It's been a challenge to build relationships with a lot of the Hmong women because there are a lot of cultural issues around gender. But now even women who were real hesitant with me two years ago are able to talk and joke with me.

There are some concrete things to take away from Jane Addams School, but it's more about a way of being with people, and the people themselves. Jane Addams School will always be a part of who I am.

Freedom

I went with Yer to take the citizenship test and to her citizenship cere-mony. I got to see how proud she was to become a US citizen. I think that has really changed my view about what citizenship means. My experiences have made me appreciate and understand it more.

A lot of the work I do at Jane Addams is about a quote from the Aborigine woman from Australia.

> "If you are here to help me, you are wasting your time. But if you have come because your liberation is bound up with mine, then come let us work together."

I see our freedom as people bound together, my freedom is bound up with Shao's freedom or Kor's freedom, and their freedom is bound up with mine. I think people are really interconnected.

Last year when I took a graduate level political theory seminar, a lot of the readings were on the concept of freedom and different concep-tions of freedom. The theory on freedom was seeing it as freedom from and freedom to. Very academic. But in my final paper, I wrote about interviewing people at Jane Addams, saying, "This is what the theory is on freedom but what does freedom mean to people?" It is so powerful to just ask someone. Someone struggling to learn Engish or someone who had to leave their county because of a war and has had many loved ones die along the way. Asking a Hmong person what freedom means is so much more powerful than asking a political theorist.

I also think freedom is bound up in choices, the ability to make dif-ferent choices. For example, I think I have had a lot of educational advantages that have given me a lot more freedom in this country. The privilege of my background and class has given me more freedom in one sense, but that is a narrow notion of freedom. There is always the freedom of how you will treat other people.

There is this book I am reading that says, "The way to do is to be." That is the way I think about my future.

I am graduating this year and I am not sure what I am going to do. I don't know if I am going to leave or stay in Minnesota but that is not as important. Sure, I am going to do things. Try to change the world. That will never change. But life is a way of being. It is always evolving, not static. That is what I am going to do.

I am going to be.

Kou Yang

I was born in Laos in 1981. My house was like the farm that people from the Jane Addams School go to. We lived in a village with maybe a thousand people in it. The village and farm were surrounded by forest. It was like an island—the woods surrounded our village the way that water surrounds an island.

In Laos, I just played like any kid. Like kids running around the street in the United States, my friends and I played together in the village.

All the families farmed the land together. My sister and mother worked on the farm with my father, and I babysat for my younger brothers and sisters. My father was a soldier before I was born, but he didn't talk about it with us.

One night we heard that the Communists were going to attack our village. At midnight, my dad and two of my uncles took us to hide in the forest. We hid in the forest for at least a month. We made tents out of banana leaves—they are big and long, so they made the best tents. We ate by killing wild animals, plus we had brought rice with us when we left the village. We drank water and coconut milk.

After about a month, we went back to the village. We heard that the Communists were not coming after all. My parents made a decision then: if that happened again, we were going to Thailand and then to America. That was our plan.

About a year later, it happened again. But this time, the Communists did attack the village. And this time we didn't have any warning. It was about two in the morning when we heard the gunfire. My dad came to wake us up, and we ran to the forest. We didn't have time to pack—we just grabbed some blankets and a little food.

My family escaped to the forest, but not everyone got away. Many people were killed. The Communists burned our houses. The houses were made of bamboo, so they burned easily and quickly. The villagers were shot.

I was six years old at that time.

□

We traveled through the jungle for about a week, on our way to the Mekong River. My dad was a hunter, so he knew the way. We ate bananas, but didn't have much other food.

I was old enough to walk. My sister also walked. My dad carried my second brother and my mother carried my third brother.

In the beginning of the trip, there were six children. But my youngest brother and sister, who were 1 year old and 1 month old, died from hunger in the woods. We had to leave them behind.

I was scared, shaking and nervous, not knowing what to do. The Communists were following us. We traveled for many days, and I don't think my father slept at all.

At the Mekong River we made a boat out of bamboo. We made one boat and my uncles made another boat. We crossed the river together, one behind the other. When we landed on the other side of the river, some Thai people were shooting at us. Then they came out and said they would not shoot at us any more.

During our crossing, our group got separated. My dad, my sister, my uncle and my grandfather got separated from us. The Thai people were there, shooting at us, and we got separated. We didn't know what had happened to them.

The Thai then took us to prison. We were all put in one room. We were there for about six months. Then a bus picked us up, and we went to the refugee camp.

We lived in the refugee camp for about three or four years. The houses in the camp had no doors.

We waited for the time when our names would be put on a list to go to the United States. We couldn't leave the camp until our names got called.

□

We came to the United States in 1991—my mother, grandmother, uncle, three brothers and sisters and I. My whole family left for the United States, except for my dad and one sister. We came directly to St. Paul, Minnesota. My aunt lived here, and she had found a church to sponsor my family.

When we first came to St. Paul, we lived on the West Side with my aunt. At that time, we couldn't go outside to play because we didn't know the neighborhood yet. We had to stay home.

There were so many new things we had never seen before, like street-lights and traffic lights. I had never seen a light switch or a shower. I didn't even know how to flush the toilet.

My aunt taught us how to use the shower, freezer, refrigerator, stove, and sink. She taught my mom and uncle, so that they could then teach us.

We heard about my father for the first time in 1992. He was living in a camp in Thailand. A few years later, my uncle came and told us my father did not want to come join our family in the United States, so my parents got divorced. My sister was in the camp also. She is married now and lives in Laos.

□

I didn't know any English when I came to the United States. But I learned it quickly in American schools. Now I know both languages. Being bilingual in this country is an unique asset. I can speak Hmong to Hmong people and English to English-speaking Americans. It's fun and it makes me more free. I don't live in a city where there is only one language, so it is essential for freedom.

I think the United States is better than Laos because we can go to school, get an education, and then find work. There is more freedom here. I'm now a sophomore at Humboldt High School. My goal is to find a good job, so I can take care of my family. At this time, I'm most interested in computers.

Hmong culture is still essential to my life. We wear traditional cloth-ing and use cultural things. Taking care of my family is the most important thing to me. When I was young, they took care of me, so now I have to give respect back to my elders. Last March, I got married. I really enjoy being married. It's better than being single. I now have a shared life with my wife.

My mother taught me that we are immigrants in this country, so we've got to be good. She tells me to stay out of gangs. She says that because we're immigrants we have to be good and work to improve Hmong culture. We must also contribute to America. I will teach my children the same way that my mother has taught me.

After family, the other thing that is important to me is helping other people and working in the community. The work at Jane Addams School with the Children's Circle is fun and. It is also good because it allows me to speak Hmong and translate for the young children and adults.

Kong Yang Thao

Growing up, I heard many stories of my parents' journey out of Laos. They left because of the war—the fighting that was going on. My father was part of the military, so after the Americans left he either had to run or fight.

My parents told me that when they were coming to the U.S., they had many troubles. Before reaching Thailand, they had to make their way through the jungle. On the trip, one of my father's toes was blown off by a land mine.

But they said that the most difficult thing was crossing the Mekong River. It was rapid and wide. They either had to take a raft or pay for a taxi boat to get across. They crossed by river taxi in about 1978 or 1979. My mother was pregnant with me at the time.

After they crossed the river they were relieved. The Thai people helped the Hmong people somewhat. My parents were in Thailand for about one year, spending time in 2 or 3 different refugee camps. I was born in one of these camps. I was 6 months old when we came to the U.S.

□

I have three brothers and two sisters. I'm the oldest. I'm 18. My brother is 17, my oldest sister is 16, my other sister is 15, and my two little brothers are 13 and 11. I have to watch over them a lot. I have to restrict how much TV they watch and how many video games they play. I tell them not to skip school or smoke or drink. My parents have their citizenship, so I'm a citizen too.

When I'm at school I feel a part of American culture, but when I'm home, I feel a part of Hmong culture. Sometimes it is hard. But my parents understand that since we go to school, we have to study. At home, because of our Hmong culture, we have chores to do, whether you are a boy or a girl.

I go to school and learn what other people in America are learning. Other students learn about the Hmong from me. But we can't really explain fully who the Hmong are. The background I know is that we fled from China about 400 years ago because of a revolution. Hmong people and the Chinese had a great war, and they drove us out of our land. That's how we landed in Laos.

When I tell my friends about Hmong culture they think it's interesting. I have a lot of friends who are other races, and to us it doesn't matter if you're Asian or White or Hispanic. We're all friends and it doesn't matter what we are—we're just all friends. To me the differences don't matter because race and color don't matter. We are all human beings, and we should treat each other as human beings.

I think being bilingual, speaking Hmong and English, is unique because most people don't know that the Hmong even exist. If I went to North Dakota or Montana and asked people what "Hmong" means, they probably would never have heard of it. I'd tell them that we came from Southeast Asia, and we came to America because of the Vietnam War. The Americans helped us.

Now, Hmong culture is a part of most of my life. I never really switched from being Hmong to being American because I have a lot of pride in being Hmong. I speak Hmong at home with my family. We still eat Hmong food, especially rice. We still celebrate Hmong New Year each year. We dress in traditional clothing, we have a lot of different activities, and we eat a lot of food.

The Hmong New Year is fun. We throw balls back and forth, and there is dancing and singing. We wear our traditional clothing. My mom is probably going to pass down our cultural clothing that she made to me and my children. I wear the clothing during New Year and at other special occasions.

Other Hmong events include soccer tournaments. That is when all the Hmong get together and have a soccer tournament against other Hmong people and other groups to see who is the best team. There is also Hmong food, music, and activities. The biggest tournament happens every summer in St. Paul around the 4th of July.

There are a lot of Hmong values that I believe in. The most important one is to live your life to the best of your ability. Everybody who came from Laos tells me that. They mean that since they worked hard for us, we should work hard for our ancestors. They have the belief that your ancestors are always with you, and they are going to look at you and think that you are either bad or good and tell your soul which path to take: the good or the bad. They will help me to take the good path.

I will help to preserve Hmong culture the same way the old folks have—by telling our stories. The stories of our last names and the stories of how people came to be. I will tell the same stories to my kids and write them down since we have a writing system now.

My mom told me the story of how we got our last names.

> There were these two gods. They had a lot of people on their world, and they all had the same last name. They didn't know who to call what because whenever they said a name, a bunch of people would come. Then all these people gathered around and told the gods to throw a rock on top of a mountain. The people stood around the mountain, and when the rock hit the mountain it split, and kept splitting as it rolled down the mountain towards the people. When it got to the people, there was a name engraved on each piece and that became their last name. The main names were Thao, Yang, Vang, and Xiong.

The best thing that my parents taught me was not to be lazy about what you are doing. They say I should always be doing something productive. My grandfather died when my father was only 10 years old. At age 11 or 12 someone trained my father to be in the military. They received supplies from the Americans. My dad had to work hard to live through all of those years. He tells us he did so much for us kids, and he just wants us to be the best we can.

My parents wish they had gone to school more when they first came to the United States. Language is the biggest obstacle to freedom for the older Hmong and anyone who hasn't gone to school.

Freedom is a big issue, but there comes a point where freedom doesn't even matter. For instance, in the United States there is a lot of freedom to do things yourself. That's a lot of freedom. But if you can't speak English then your freedom is restricted, and you can't really do much.

I have been working at the Jane Addams School for a few months. It's going great. I like to work in the Children Circle. The kids are nosy and playful. It's fun. It's also worth the time to work with the adults as well as the kids. They're trying to get out of the prison of the language barrier and learn English. Jane Addams School doesn't teach people to abandon their cultures. They're teaching people to learn the American way and to keep their culture because the Americans are learning a lot from the Hmong too.

Kai Lee

In Laos, life was free.

We could do whatever we wanted. Everyday, my mom and my cousins would go to work in the fields. We lived high up in the mountains, so the fields were on the sides of steep, steep hills. We had to work very hard because farming was our only source of food and income.

There were trees all around us, and we loved to climb them. My family didn't have any money to buy toys, but my dad used to take things from the forest, trees and plants, and make toys for us. He made wooden swords and slingshots. My cousins and I would fight imaginary battles with our swords. We used the slingshots to catch squirrels and birds to eat. We used to tie the slingshots around our heads and then climb up the trees. We could see everything from up there!

My dad was a soldier. He fought with the Chao Fa.* After a while, he had to leave our family because we were threatened by the fighting in the war. If he stayed with us, we would all be in danger, so he and the other men in our village went into hiding.

□

Eventually, our family, our entire village, fled to safety.

We began our journey to Thailand, taking only what we could carry with us. We brought one pot and one pan. My mom carried my younger brother, who was about four years old, on her back, as well as our clothes and blankets. My older sister and I were old enough to walk—I was about six and she was about nine.

We were scared. The air around us was filled with fear and tension. We were afraid of making any noise because then the Communists would find us. If a child cried, other people would threaten to kill it, to slice its throat.

On the way there, we saw many terrible things—killings, dead bodies. My dad was shot in the back by the communist soldiers. It was horrible to see my dad shot right in front of me. He still has that scar today.

Once we got to Thailand, we stayed in a refugee camp near the border with Laos. I started first grade in this camp. I remember learning the alphabet. Our teacher would hit our fingers with a ruler if we spelled the words wrong.

□

After four or five months, my family was moved to Phanat Nikhom.* I remember this camp very well. We shared a house with another family, and it was really crowded.

I saw new things in Phanat Nikhom, things I had never seen before. Sometimes, they showed movies—on a big screen, not on a TV. I thought this was so cool. It was fun and exciting. I had never seen anything like it. But we had to pay to see the movies, and my family did not have very much money. Our cousins in the United States used to send us some money, but it was limited, so I was only able to go to the movies twice.

One of the things that my brothers, my cousins and I loved to do was to go fishing. We used to throw rocks into the water to catch fish and crabs. We could only go fishing in a small creek inside the camp because the camp was surrounded with barbed wire, and we weren't allowed to go outside.

* Translated as "Prince of the Sky," the Chao Fa is a mystical group originating in the early 1900's. After the Communists took control of Laos in 1975, the Chao Fa became the major Hmong guerilla group that continued to fight for freedom. (For more on the Chao Fa, see Jane Hamilton-Merritt's "Tragic Mountains: the Hmong, the Americans, and the Secret Wars for Laos, 1942–1992.")
* Phanat Nikhom Refugee Processing Center, located in Central Thailand, was the final stop for refugees before they resettled in a third country. At Phanat Nikhom, all refugees going to the United States participated in six months of English language instruction and cultural orientation classes.

One day when we were fishing in the creek, we accidentally went outside the wire. The creek led to a concrete tunnel, and we followed the water through the tunnel. Suddenly we were outside of the camp. We were having fun, so we started to walk further from the camp. We hadn't noticed that there was a Thai guard near us, but he saw us. He stood in front of us, with his legs open wide and his hands on his hips—he was angry! We were so scared! My brothers and cousins were so scared that they ran away, back towards the camp. I ran and hid behind a cement wall.

The guard hadn't seen how many of us there were, so I thought that he wouldn't come looking for me. But we had left our sandals on the other side of the tunnel, and he went back and counted our shoes. I couldn't go back to the tunnel because he would catch me. I couldn't stay where I was hiding because he would come and find me. So I ran and ran in the opposite direction. I was so scared because I knew that if we were caught, my family would lose the chance to go to the United States. I ran to a Thai store, a place that played music, where there were many Thai kids. I sat down and tried to blend in with them. Finally the soldier left, and I sneaked back into the camp. We never went outside the barbed wire again.

□

Soon after that, my family left Thailand for the United States. We flew to Fresno, California, where we lived for the next ten years. I started second grade in Fresno—I don't know why I started in second, maybe because I had been in first grade in Thailand, maybe because of my age. I was about eight years old then.

My first year of school was terrible. I really hated the food at school, so I would bring my own food from home. My friends would always ask me for my food, but I never wanted to give it away because I couldn't stand to eat the school food.

School was difficult for me because I couldn't speak English very well. I had two friends, two Hmong friends, who used to help me. They would translate for me, but they were screwy. They used to teach me bad words. They would tell me what to say, and I'd be saying these bad words, but I had no idea. They thought it was funny. Once I had to ask the teacher if I could go to the bathroom, and my friends told me what to say—bad things. The teacher got so mad. She made me go stand in the corner, but I had no idea what I had done. What had I said that made her so angry?

Later, when I learned more English, I found out what I had been saying, and I felt bad. I was embarrassed.

In third grade, I cheated a lot in school. I still had a lot of language struggles, and I didn't understand what was going on. When the teacher would look away, I would look at the other students' papers. I knew it was wrong, but I just didn't understand.

In fourth grade I became the target of the class bully—Luis Sanchez. I was scared the entire year. I was always a quiet kid. I had perfect attendance, and the teacher liked me. We had a mixed class, fourth and fifth graders together. One day it was really hot, and after the bell rang we were all waiting in line at the drinking fountain. Luis was drinking water, I was behind him, and another girl, Maria, was behind me. Luis was taking so long that Maria hit him on the back to get him to hurry up. But Luis thought it was me.

He was after me all the time after that. He would bully me and call me names—"Chinese eyes." At recess, he would grab me, push me into the restroom, and beat me up. I didn't know who to tell. I had some friends, but they were not Hmong and I didn't feel completely comfortable with them. Also I was afraid that if I told anybody, he would beat me up even worse.

□

Then I switched schools and things got much better. In junior high I worked so hard. In both seventh and eighth grade I had perfect attendance and a 4.0 grade point average. My parents were so happy, so proud of me. At our graduation, my best friend Noy and I were the top two students in the class. I was really proud. We were equals in school, but she had been born in the US and I hadn't. I had worked hard to catch up with her.

I was so happy and proud that my hard work was helping me get ahead. In ninth grade, I was one of only two freshmen in Algebra II, and that was a good feeling. But then I had my first girlfriend, and my GPA fell quickly! It was a really bad experience.

I didn't know anything about girls, and she was not a good one. My friends told me that she was a player, but I didn't listen. One of my friends really wanted me to get out of my relationship with her. He wanted to prove to me that she was a player. So one day he took me to her house and told me to hide in the bushes. Then he came outside with her and she kissed him—right in front of me! I know that he was trying to help me see what a bad person she was, but that was a terrible experience. It was so painful to see that.

After that, I worked really hard in school. I took nine classes my sophomore year. I was in school from six in the morning until eight at night. Then I would come home and do my homework. Sometimes I stayed up until two in the morning studying. I also went to summer school every year between seventh and tenth grades. This helped me to make up for lost time, for having to learn a new language.

Last August, my family moved to St. Paul because Minnesota has better job opportunities, and now we're closer to my cousins. I live with my mom, my dad, my five brothers and two sisters. My older sister is married and lives in California. I got married two weeks ago, so now my wife, Tshua, lives with us, too.

One of the things I dream about for Hmong people is unity, but there are many things that separate us, that keep us from being one people. For one thing, in the United States we have to worry not only about our own culture, but also about how to survive in this country. And survival is more important—we need to go to school and to work in order to make it here. So we spend more time within American culture than we do in keeping our own traditions. Also, there are some things, some parts of our culture and traditions that we can't do in America.

Another thing that separates us is the clashes between the clans. Some of the older people cannot let go of old conflicts, things that happened with our ancestors generations ago. They still hold onto this. This is really bad, but they can't control their feelings.

□

Gangs are another problem that our community faces. In my opinion, gangs wouldn't have started without hate. The Hmong gangs in the United States have to do with the clan rivalries that have been carried down through the generations. The elders keep bringing these up— "Oh, so and so did this to our clan"—and the young people hear this. It has an effect on them.

But I think that gangs also grow here because the government is not strict enough, the rules and the punishment are not strict enough. In Laos, our houses were only made from twigs and straw, but when you left your house to go to the fields, no one would touch your valuables. You didn't have to worry. There were no gangs because there were stricter rules. Young people did not want to do the wrong thing.

But in the United States, when a young person sees something bad or wrong, they want to do it. They want to experience that bad thing. They want the challenge. I think the punishment is not great enough for them to stop doing those things.

Also, parents here are not strict enough. The older people are afraid of the laws in America. They think that if they physically discipline their children they will go to jail. They think that kids have more authority than parents do. And the kids know that their parents can't control them. This makes them want to have fun, to have total freedom. Some parents just give up. They don't know how to discipline their kids anymore, and the laws don't help them.

If we had stayed in Laos, things would be different.

But I can see and understand both sides. At night I like to think about different things, to reminisce, to try to understand things. And first I will agree with one side and think that this is the "right" side. But then I will see that there's a "left" side too. And I get caught in the middle. I think there has to be a solution that comes from both sides. For example, the police would lose their jobs if there were no gangs, so they're caught up in it too. The gangs and violence are a cycle that they play a part in, too.

I have a friend in California who is in a gang. He's been locked up so many times. He told me how he started. There was this girl who liked him, but he didn't like her. He wouldn't talk to her. Her boyfriend was in a gang, and he found out that she liked my friend and got jealous. He came up to my friend and started saying bad stuff to him. My friend didn't want to lose his manhood, his coolness. He is really short-tempered, so he fought him. Then that guy's gang came after him. Again and again. He changed schools, but they followed him. Eventually, he had no way out. He joined a different gang for protection and to get back at them. It wasn't something that he wanted, but he fell into it.

He didn't think he had a choice.

He says being in the gang is about having freedom and having a family, but he always tells other people not to follow in his footsteps. He tells us that it isn't worth it. That it is a bad path to follow. He has to watch his back at all times.

□

Hmong culture is a very important part of my life. Being a Hmong boy, it's hard enough going through life thinking about how to survive in America. It's even harder when I think about how to survive in two cultures at the same time. It's so hard trying to keep what's left of my Hmong identity, trying to preserve it so that it will not perish.

One night I thought, "What if one day we have totally forgotten everything? What if we become so Americanized that we just become another part of America?"

I see that other races are finding a way to survive in the "melting pot," but their cultures are vanishing. It's already happening to us. Our people are trying hard to survive in a world totally different from that of our native land. We don't farm to feed our families anymore. We don't travel for days on foot just to get to the lowlands or the capital. There have been major changes in our lives.

I see so many youngsters out there who are lost, who have already forgotten who they are. Many Hmong kids don't speak our language, eat our parents' food, learn about our traditions, or listen when the elders tell folk tales and stories. They'd rather go play or go to parties. So our culture, our traditions, are disappearing.

Every time a Hmong elder dies without passing on their talents, another thing is lost for us. It might be just a small thing here or there, but it will all add up.

I fear that one day my identity as being Hmong will be lost forever, like an animal that has gone extinct. When something is extinct, you can't bring it back. Of course, there are always museums, but that doesn't mean as much as when it was still alive and healthy. The same concept applies to the Hmong identity. We are slowly forgetting who we are and where we are from.

The older people are dying each day and the younger generations haven't had the chance to learn everything that they need to learn. One day we will lose everything that defines us. When that time comes we will not quite be American, and we will not be Hmong either. We will be a people who is in between, who only knows a little of both.

Then we will speak English fluently, but will have lost our native tongue. Our faces will be Hmong, people will say we are Hmong, but our hearts will no longer be. Maybe one day we will have to hire someone else, someone of another race, to teach us about our culture. Historians and anthropologists will know more than us, the ones who should know, who should learn more, but who have given up.

I have never seen an application for employment or college that listed "Hmong" as a defined race. It is hurtful to me to know that not only are we minorities here, many people have never even heard of a people called "Hmong."

□

There are just so many things going through my mind as I see my people struggling in this huge world. We need time. Our parents don't have the education to get decent jobs, so they end up working overtime or else work two or three jobs. They don't have time to spend with their kids, teaching them about the culture.

I make a big deal about the Pha Hau* writing system because we need to have our own written language. It can help us to redefine, to reclaim, our vocabulary that is getting lost. There are a lot of words that younger Hmong people don't understand, and if they don't understand them, they don't say them. So these words just get lost. I volunteer to teach at the Hmong Language Institute in St. Paul, to help boys and girls learn about our language and culture. This is one way to keep our Hmong identity alive. But I wish there were something I could do to get people together. To get them united

□

Even though I spend the majority of my time within American culture, I carry my Hmong culture with me in many ways. It is a part of my daily life. In the morning we—my brothers, sisters, Tshua and I—get up and cook for our parents. This is what our ancestors did too. We have a saying that "parents raise children in time of need." They need us to be there for them. After school we cook again. And on Saturday and Sunday, we cook three meals.

We are happy to do this for our parents. Sooner or later, they will

---

* Pha Hau is a written system of the Hmong language developed in the 1960's by the Chao Fa leader, Yang Shong Lue. (For more information see William Allen Smalley's "Mother of Writing: the Origin and Development of a Hmong Messianic Script.")

be gone and we won't have the opportunity to do this for them. This is one way we can show them that we love them.

We also wear things to show that we are Hmong—like my necklace or Tshua's bracelet. Or these strings around our wrists. We wear them after weddings or "ua neeb" ceremonies.* And this red string that I wear is even more important to me. This comes not just from my family, but from my clan.* Every once in a while the leader of our clan, the Lee's, will have a big party. He will call together everyone in the clan. It could be a long time between these parties—maybe once every ten years. They tie these strings around our wrists for good luck and health. If it does not fall off, then it will stay on forever. I will never cut it off.

Our family is very important to us, and we love them very much. But we don't say, "I love you." Well, now I see some people who say this, but only a few. Sometimes our mother will tell us. But mostly we don't say it. We don't need to say it, we just know that our family loves us. I think too that if you hear "I love you" so many times, it loses its meaning. If you hear it once every ten years, it means much more to you.

□

The importance of Hmong culture to me doesn't mean that I don't want to be a part of American culture. In a way I feel like I'm a part of American culture and in some ways not. I feel exposed to it everyday, and I try to become a part of it. But it takes time. We are in it everyday, speaking and listening to English at school, on the radio and TV. We are so exposed to it that we get used to it.

There are some things about American culture that I do want to practice or learn. For example, I think there are some things I would like about American weddings. I don't like to drink, but at Hmong weddings there is a lot of drinking. The family says they give you a lot to drink to show you that they love you, that they want you to take care of their daughter. But what if I get so drunk and sick that I can't take care of her? I don't like all that drinking. I wonder why we can't do it the American way—exchange rings and then have a big party where everyone comes. I think it would be a better way to start a life together.

Also, I have a problem sometimes with the dowry. I heard about an example in San Diego where people just went too far. There was a man and a woman, both of them doctors, who fell in love and wanted to get married. The woman's family charged $20,000 for the man to marry her. I think this is a case where people have gone too far because of greed.

---

* Literally, "call shaman," an "ua neeb" is a shamanic ceremony. Part of this ceremony involves tying white strings around the wrists of family members to keep their souls connected to their bodies. At wedding ceremonies, strings are tied around the bride and groom to tie their souls to the man's clan.
* Hmong society is divided into around 20 "clans" (xeem in Hmong). Clans include a male ancestor, his sons and unmarried daughters, and the children of his sons. In the United States, the Hmong clan name is used as the equivalent of a "last name." Marriage between members of the same clan is strictly taboo.

So there are some things we could learn from American culture. It's not that we don't want to assimilate, it's just hard for the older people because they are confused. They are scared, worried about the new things that they encounter. Again, I don't blame them for it because they never got a good education or someone to teach them. Everything evolves and changes as time changes. Sometimes those changes are good. In order to survive, one must move with time. If you stop, time will pass you by—you will be lost in time. However, changing with time doesn't mean that you must forget about your own identity.

□

My parents have taught me very important lessons. Most important-ly, they taught me themselves—they showed me what they want me to be simply by being who they are. They showed me by example. They also emphasize the importance of education. They are very strict about it. Actually, my dad is strict, and my mom is more loving, more sensitive. I think it's the perfect combination; it's balanced. If both parents are too lenient, the kids could get spoiled. If both are very strict, the kids can get spoiled in another way. But my parents have a good balance.

They stress education because they never had the chance to go to school. They want their children to have better lives. They want to know that our futures are secure. My mom told me that when her time comes, she will not want to go if our futures are not secure, but if she knows that we will have good futures, she will be happy to go. She also puts a lot of stress on my leading by example. As the oldest son, I have to be a role model for my younger brothers and sisters. If I drop out of school, the younger kids could follow. My parents want all of us to at least finish high school, but preferably to finish four years of college. They want me to be a doctor or a lawyer. There are no other options.

My dad always says, "No one can love you more than you love yourself; no one can help you more than you help yourself." My fresh-man year, when I wasn't doing so well in school, he told me this every-day. I got so sick of hearing it. I'd say, "I understand! I get the point!" But he really believes in this, and he has taught this to us. So from my dad I learned the importance of hard work.

My mom taught me about love and compassion. She showed me the importance of loving others, of forgiveness. She taught me about her heart.

I guess you could say that my parents, then, gave us their two personalities.

□

There is so much that I want to teach to my children. I want to teach them everything there is to be known. I will teach them about Hmong culture—about wedding ceremonies, memorial ceremonies, "ua neeb" ceremonies. And if I can't teach them, then I will find someone who can. They have to learn these things because they are basic to our culture. They must stay. If we lose them, what will come next?

But I worry that I won't be able to teach my children all there is to know about Hmong culture. I'm still learning things now, but I won't get half of it because it's disappearing so fast. So I won't be able to give them everything.

□

I think that being a refugee and being Hmong in America puts me in a different position than many people. I have experienced a lot of things

JOYCE YAMAMOTO

that other people haven't. I can also relate to many people and say, "Oh, I've experienced that" or "I know what that's like."

And I feel like I'm bilingual, and also bicultural. It's not just about reading, writing, or speaking, it's about knowing different cultures. I even change personalities. When I'm around my American friends, I'm more outgoing because they are. When I'm with my Hmong friends, I'm quieter, because they are generally more shy. Both ways are fun; they're just different.

□

Working at the Jane Addams School has become an important part of my life in Minnesota. When I first came here, I didn't know anyone. Then I met Na at Humboldt and he introduced me to Jane Addams School. He told me it was a place where I could help out, could work with Hmong people. In Fresno, I had worked at a place that serves food to homeless people. So I wanted to find a way to help the community here. I also thought that at Jane Addams I could make friends and learn more about Minnesota. But it turned out to be more than just making friends. I lost my shyness there quickly because of the whole atmosphere– it's a "we." People ask my opinion. I can contribute what I know. We are a family.

I stay at Jane Addams School because it feels good to work with other people. I am making a difference. It's not an obligation for me. Sometimes I can't wait to get there. I wait for the school day to be over just so we can get there. I know that our being there is important to the Hmong elders. They really need us. For some of them, their only hope is to come to Jane Addams School. And for us, spending time there is better than staying at home or just hanging out. And it feels good when people compliment you, when you know that what you're doing matters to them.

The work Jane Addams School is doing for the Hmong veterans is really important. Even though it may not mean much to others, the government should recognize that there were Hmong who served and died fighting in the war. It would be so special to the Hmong veterans. They took a lot of pride in that war, fighting alongside the US soldiers. Whenever they talk, they stress this because it's the only memory of why we are here today. They want someone to listen to the stories of how they fought, where they fought. Someone to give them feedback about their efforts, to compliment them. Wouldn't anyone?

Jane Addams School is important to me because I am a "Hmong American." This means I can't be just one or the other; I have to be both. All day long when I am in school, I am American. At home and in the community, I am Hmong. But at Jane Addams, I can be both. I can teach people, older people, what I know about being American, and I can learn from them what it means to be Hmong. It gives us the time that we need together to learn from each other.

□

I am really happy to be married. Now I can concentrate more on school—I don't have to worry about finding a girlfriend or going to parties. Tshua is so cool. She understands the elders and Hmong traditions. She has had similar experiences as me, so we understand each other. We can talk about everything, and we have empathy for each other. We share great times together, and we want to have similar lives. She's also a really good cook.

In Hmong culture, there are two ways that you can get married. The first is to go to the girl's house and ask her family for their permission to marry their daughter. The second is to take their daughter to your house and then call them up and say, "Don't worry. Your daughter is with me now. I love her and will take care of her for the rest of her life. If you need anything, we will always be there for you."

Tshua and I got married the second way.

In Laos, sometimes the man would take the woman against her will—kidnapping. I don't understand that. If she doesn't love you, what's the point? You don't want to live a life of loving someone who doesn't love you back. That's a sad, sad feeling. That's a sad, sad man. Tshua and I talked about everything beforehand. Otherwise, I never would have done it.

□

I see many things in our future. In the short-term, I see college, finishing college. I just got accepted to the University of Minnesota and I'm really excited to go. I want to be a double-major in computer engineering and teaching. I will prove people wrong who say that because I am married I won't go far.

I have always dreamed of buying a big house. I want to be successful. This means being happy, having financial resources, a secure job to support my whole family. People say money can't buy you happiness, but it does help.

Most of all, I want to live my life with no regrets